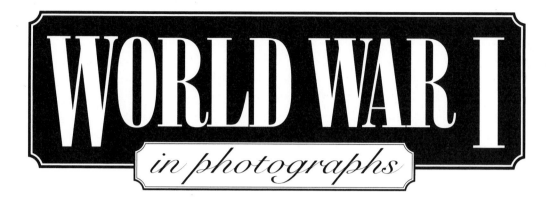

WORLD WAR I
in photographs

Above: German storm troops in action on the Western front in 1918.

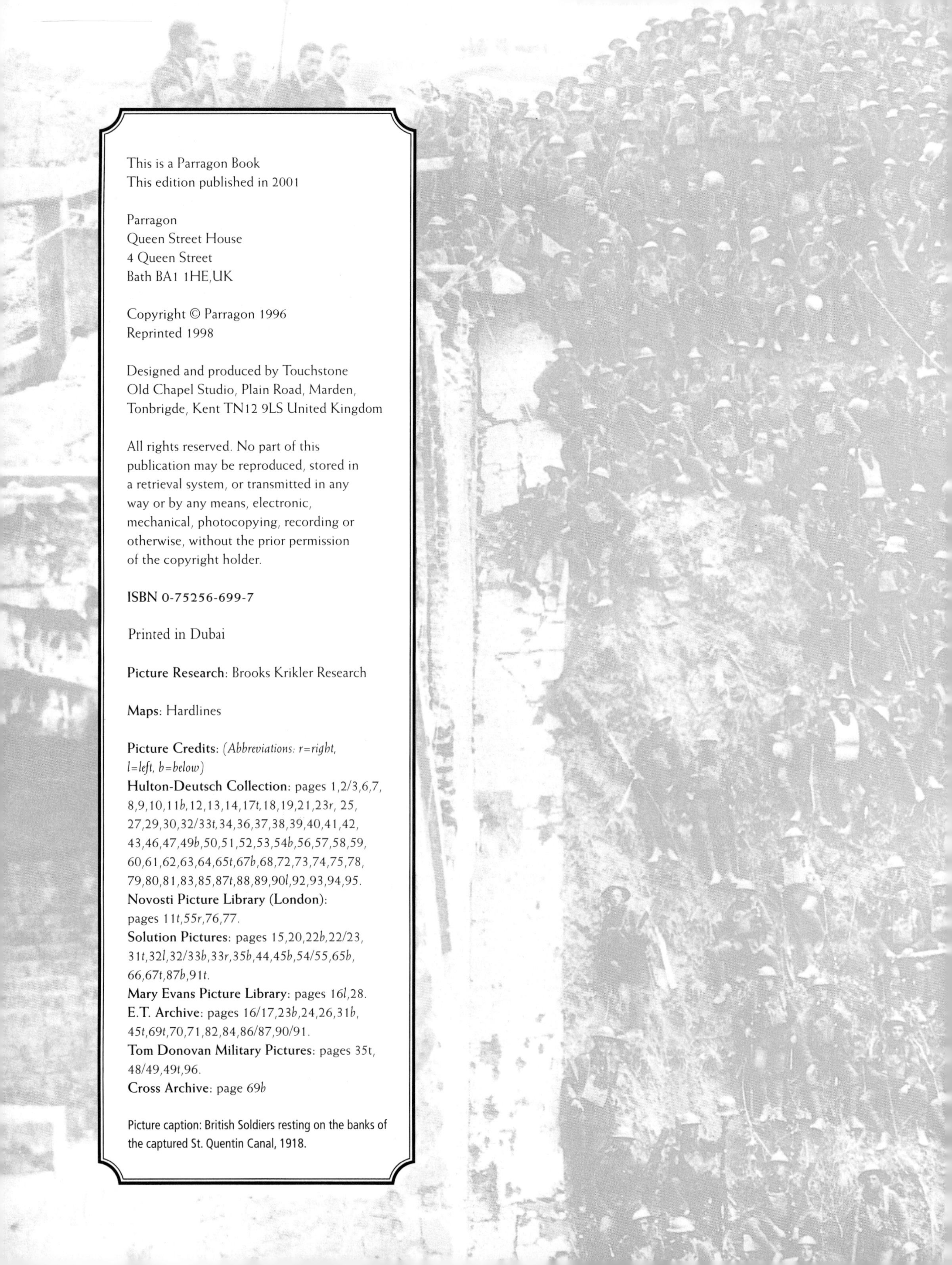

This is a Parragon Book
This edition published in 2001

Parragon
Queen Street House
4 Queen Street
Bath BA1 1HE, UK

Designed and produced by Touchstone
Old Chapel Studio, Plain Road, Marden,
Tonbrigde, Kent TN12 9LS United Kingdom

ISBN 0-75256-699-7

Printed in Dubai

Picture Research: Brooks Krikler Research

Maps: Hardlines

Picture Credits: *(Abbreviations: r=right,
l=left, b=below)*
Hulton-Deutsch Collection: pages 1,2/3,6,7,
8,9,10,11b,12,13,14,17t,18,19,21,23r, 25,
27,29,30,32/33t,34,36,37,38,39,40,41,42,
43,46,47,49b,50,51,52,53,54b,56,57,58,59,
60,61,62,63,64,65t,67b,68,72,73,74,75,78,
79,80,81,83,85,87t,88,89,90l,92,93,94,95.
Novosti Picture Library (London):
pages 11t,55r,76,77.
Solution Pictures: pages 15,20,22b,22/23,
31t,32l,32/33b,33r,35b,44,45b,54/55,65b,
66,67t,87b,91t.
Mary Evans Picture Library: pages 16l,28.
E.T. Archive: pages 16/17,23b,24,26,31b,
45t,69t,70,71,82,84,86/87,90/91.
Tom Donovan Military Pictures: pages 35t,
48/49,49t,96.
Cross Archive: page 69b

Picture caption: British Soldiers resting on the banks of
the captured St. Quentin Canal, 1918.

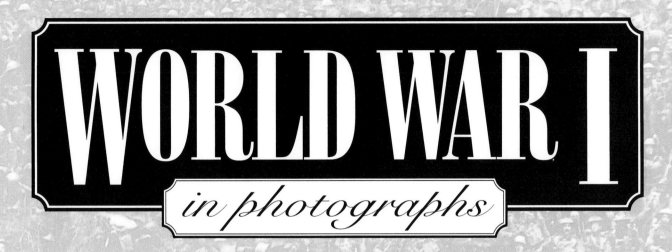

WORLD WAR I
in photographs

ROBIN CROSS

WORLD WAR I 1914–1918

	Neutral states throught the war
	Central powers at the outbreak of war
	Entente powers at the outbreak of the war
	States which joined central powers
	Frontlines November 1918
	Maximum advance of the central powers
	Frontlines August 1914
	Neutral states which later joined the Entente
	Russo–German border early 1915

NORWAY
SWEDEN
NORTH SEA
DENMARK
GREAT BRITAIN
St Petersburg
Dorport
Pskov
Moscow
RUSSIA
Riga
Dvinsk
Voronezh
London Amsterdam
Copenhagen
Hamburg
Berlin
Tilsit
Vilna
Tannenberg
Minsk
Begorod
Baranovichi
R. Volga
Calais
Cologne
GERMAN EMPIRE
Warsaw
Gomel
Millerova
Verdun
Metz
Munich
Prague
Pinsk
R. Dnieper
R. Donets
R. Don
Paris
FRANCE
Vienna
AUSTRIA HUNGARY
Odessa
Azov
R. Volga
Berne
Lyon SWITZERLA
Budapest
R. Danube
Kerch
Petrovsk
Milan
Trieste
Belgrade
ROMANIA
Sebastopol
Tiflis
Baku
Venice
MONTE NEGRO
SERBIA BULGARIA
BLACK SEA
Batumi
Lisbon Madrid
Marseilles
ALBANIA
Sofia
Tréblizond
Erzipean
R. Tagus SPAIN
CORSICA
Thessalonika
Constantinople
Bitlis
Rome
Gallipoli
Ankara
OTTOMAN EMPIRE
Rawanduz
PERSIA
SARDINIA
SICILY
Athens
Aleppo
Kitri
Tekrit
Ramadi
Bagdad
MEDITERRANEAN SEA
Damascus
ALGERIA
LIBYA
EGYPT Cairo
Jerusalem
ARABIA

THE WESTERN FRONT

Amsterdam
The Hague NETHERLANDS
Rotterdam
GREAT BRITAIN
NORTH SEA
London
Zeebrugge
Antwerp
Dunkirk Ostend
R. Yser Ypres
Armentières
R. Rhine
Messines
Mons Namur R. Meuse
Loos Cambrai R. Sambre
Artois region
Ardennes region
Mainz
Picardy region Arras
Charleroi
R. Somme
Noyon Mézières Stenay
Amiens
Craonne Sedan
Thionville
Compiègne Soissons Argonne region
Verdun
Metz Lemberg
R. Oise Reims
Lorraine region
Château- Montfaucon St Mihiel
R. Seine Thierry
Nancy
R. Marne
Paris
Epinal
R. Seine
Belfort
SWITZERLAND
ENGLISH CHANNEL

- - - German advance 1914
—— Trench warfare line 1917
- - - Farthest German advance 1918
—— Front line at Armistice

CONTENTS

THE FIRST SHOTS

ON 28 JUNE 1914, the Archduke Franz Ferdinand of Austria, heir to the monarchy of the Habsburgs, visited the Bosnian town of Sarajevo to inspect Austrian troops there. Bosnia, and its sister province Herzegovina, were former Turkish possessions which had been annexed by Austria-Hungary in 1908. Many of its Serb inhabitants were bitterly resentful at not being allowed to join Serbia, their native state. One of them, a grammar school student named Gavrilo Princip, assassinated the Archduke and his wife as they rode through the streets of Sarajevo in an open car.

On 28 July, Austria-Hungary retaliated by declaring war on Serbia, a diplomatic rather than a military move as it would take several weeks for the Austrians to mobilise. The Russians then stepped in on the side of the Serbs, their fellow-Slavs. The Russians could not allow the Serbs to be humiliated, nor permit the Austrians and their German ally to dominate the Balkans and, by extension, Russia's access to the Mediterranean through the Dardanelles Straits. Russia mobilized on 29 July 1914.

Left: The last picture of the Archduke Franz Ferdinand and his wife, taken shortly before his assassination in Sarajevo on 28 June 1914. The couple had survived a bomb thrown at their car on the way to the town hall, but were shot by Gavrilo Princip as they returned to the railway station. Their car had taken a wrong turning and was reversing when Princip stepped forward to fire the fatal shots. The Archduke's last words were 'It is nothing'.

On 1 August, Germany declared war on Russia and mobilised. Russia's ally France also mobilised on the same day. On 3 August, at 6.45pm, Germany declared war on France. The next day Germany invaded Belgium, which had been declared a neutral country by the Treaty of London in 1839. Now the British were drawn in. They sent Germany an ultimatum asking her to withdraw from Belgium. There was no reply and by midnight on 4 August, Britain and Germany were at war. The British had been the only nation to declare war on Germany rather than the other way round. As the British Foreign Secretary, Sir Edward Grey, waited for the midnight deadline, he remarked, *'The lamps are going out all over Europe. We shall not see them lit again in our time'.*

Left: Austria mobilizes. Men and boys cross Franz Josef Square in Vienna to join up. On 28 July Austria had declared war on Serbia. The German Kaiser Wilhelm II approved of the Austrian move, confident that Russia would not intervene. But the wheels of war were now in unstoppable motion.

Below: Before the storm. Warships of the Royal Navy visit the German naval base at Kiel while a Zeppelin hovers overhead. In 1912 Graf von Zeppelin's commercial airship company DELAG had been secretly informed that its crews were to join the military reserve and participate in regular exercises with the Army and the Navy.

WAR BY TIMETABLE

WHY DID Gavrilo Princip's shots in Sarajevo lead to a world war? At first the incident was hardly noted in Britain. Kaiser Wilhelm II of Germany did not believe that Russia would intervene on behalf of the Serbs. He was not going to let the crisis interfere with his planned holiday cruise. What went wrong?

Over the tangle of great power rivalry in Europe, with its shifting alliances and brutal jockeying for imperial position, lay the shadow of the huge conscript armies assembled by the continental powers in the late 19th century. Industrial muscle and expanding populations had produced deep pools of manpower which could be mobilized as acts of political policy to achieve national ends. The politicians calculated on their deterrent effect to avoid war, but did not anticipate that these great armies, accumulated to keep the peace, would once mobilized, propel the nations into war by their own fearful weight.

The staff of each army had prepared detailed war plans in advance. Those of Germany and France involved the use of precise railway timetables for the mass movement of men and material. The technological gears that made these movements possible could not be thrown into reverse by the politicians, who at this point had irrevocably surrendered control to their generals. In the first fortnight of August 1914, some 20 million men – nearly 10 per cent of the populations of the combatant states – donned uniforms and took the trains to war. All believed that they would be back home, *'before the leaves fell'*.

Left: General Sir Douglas Haig with Lord Haldane (right) in March 1914. Four months later Haig was on his way to France as commander of the British Expeditionary Force's I Corps. As Secretary of State for War, 1905-12, Haldane presided over a programme to modernize the British Army on European lines, creating a British Expeditionary Force (BEF) and a Territorial Reserve (TA) to provide reserves. Haldane's reforms ensured that the BEF crossed the Channel speedily and efficiently in August 1914.

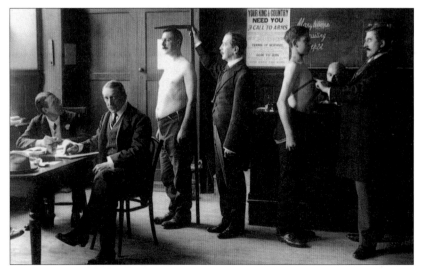

Above: They thought it would be over by Christmas. Crowds in Trafalgar Square cheer Britain's declaration of war. Along the Mall and outside Buckingham Palace a throng of people sang 'God Save the King'.

Right: British volunteers undergo a medical examination at Marylebone grammar school in London. There were many rejects, the overall standard of health among working men being low, particularly in industrial areas. The youngster on the right looks well below the minimum age of 19.

THE BALANCE OF POWER

O N THE eve of war the German Army, drawing on a reserve of 4.3 million trained men, was organised in 25 army corps comprising 87 infantry and 11 cavalry divisions. The front-line army was supported by 32 highly capable reserve divisions. The German cavalry, diluted with light infantry to increase firepower, proved a disappointment in the opening phase of the war, as did the field artillery, with its standard equipment of the obsolescent 3-inch gun. The great strength of German artillery lay in its heavy guns for use in the field, particularly the 5.9-inch howitzer.

The polyglot army of Germany's Austro-Hungarian ally, with its 49 infantry divisions and 11 of cavalry, was more of a liability than an asset. Over 50 per cent of its troops were Slavs, Czechs and Italians – men whose natural sympathies lay with Austria's enemies rather than the Dual Monarchy. This was a factor behind some of the more spectacular Austrian collapses of the war. The fragility of the Austrian armies was exacerbated by the Chief of the Austrian General Staff, Field Marshal von Hötzendorf, whose strategic reach generally exceeded his grasp.

When mobilised, the Russians would field 114 infantry and 36 cavalry divisions, the legendary 'steamroller'. Although much had been done to revive it following the humiliating defeat by Japan in 1905, the Russian Army remained poorly equipped, with reserves of ammunition and rifles in short supply, desperately short of competent officers at the lower levels and riddled with corruption at the top

The French Army had made a remarkable recovery from the utter ruin of 1871 to field 75 infantry and 10 cavalry divisions infused with the doctrine of all-out attack developed after the disaster of the Franco-Prussian War. Symbolic of this spirit was the infantry's retention of conspicuous red trousers and heavy, dark blue coats. They were not replaced by 'horizon blue' uniforms until 1915.

Above: Austrian troops bid farewell to their wives and sweethearts. The weakness of the polyglot Austro-Hungarian Army was revealed in its opening campaign of the war, when on 11 August it invaded Serbia. The Serbs threw the Austrians out and in turn invaded southern Hungary. It was the first of many Austrian defeats. The most reliable element in the Austro-Hungarian Army was its heavy artillery, the massive Skoda howitzers, which played an important part in German plans.

Right: A newsreel camera catches Russian infantry on the way to the front in 1914. The Russian army was a clumsy giant, short of equipment and competent officers. But its illiterate peasant soldiery showed remarkable endurance throughout the war, supported by a tenacious artillery arm and the savage dash of the Cossack cavalry across the endless plains of eastern Europe.

Below: Backbone of the French artillery, the quick-firing 75mm field gun introduced in 1897. By 1918 some 17,000 '75s' had been produced. Its hydro-pneumatic recoil system made the '75' very stable when fired and its quick-acting breech mechanism gave it a firing rate of up to 20 rounds a minute. It could throw a 12-pound high-explosive or 16-pound shrapnel shell up to 10,000 yards. However, French offensive doctrine meant that the '75' was not ideally suited to trench warfare, and the shells it fired were too light to pose a threat to heavily defended positions.

From their small regular Army, the British supplied six infantry divisions and one and a half of cavalry for the Expeditionary Force to France. Compared with its European counterparts, the BEF was lavishly motorized, its 75,000 men supported by 1,485 motor vehicles of all kinds. The cavalry had useful mounted infantry training. The artillery's lack of heavy guns was balanced by the excellent 18-pounder field gun. However, the Army contained few officers with any experience of commanding large formations of men.

THE SCHLIEFFEN PLAN

IN THE 1890s the Chief of the German General Staff, Field Marshal Alfred von Schlieffen, turned his attention to Germany's fundamental strategic problem: how to cope with a war on two fronts; against Russia in the East and France in the West.

Schlieffen's solution was to seek a swift decision against France with the bulk of his forces while holding the Russians in check as they slowly mobilized. He intended to draw the bulk of the French Army towards the Rhine by leaving this sector weakly defended. The weight of the German blow was to be delivered in a swinging right hook through Belgium and northern France. Its extreme right would pass south of Paris, crossing the Seine near Rouen to take the French armies in the rear, pinning them against the Lorraine fortresses and the Swiss frontier.

Left: Alfred von Schlieffen (1833-1913), the German army's Chief of Staff, 1891-1906, who devised the plan to deal with war against Russia in the East and France in the West. France was to be overrun in the minimum time through the encirclement of her armies, making maximum use of railways, while a holding operation was mounted against the slowly mobilizing Russians in the East.

Right: In scorching summer heat, German infantry advance into Belgium in August 1914. The destruction of much of the railway system by the Belgian army meant that the critical distance between marching columns and railheads stretched to about 80 miles. Marching at a pace of 30 miles a day, the men of German First Army were reaching the point of exhaustion before the serious fighting had begun. There was no motor transport to help them. The five northern German armies operating between Luxembourg and Brussels had only 500 motor lorries between them.

After Schlieffen's retirement in 1906, the Plan was steadily watered down by his successor, von Moltke. The German left wing was strengthened at the expense of the all-important right. In August 1914 the Schlieffen Plan's ratio of forces between north and south had fallen from 7:1 to 3:1, depriving the right wing in the north of the strength to execute a complete encircling movement. Although the Plan had become unworkable, it was to exercise an inexorable influence on the inception and opening phase of the war.

Helmuth von Moltke, von Schlieffen's successor. He ignored von Schlieffen's dying words — 'Keep the right strong' — and fatally weakened the right wing of the German offensive against northern France, ensuring that it lacked the strength to accomplish a complete encirclement of the French armies. On 14 September 1914 he was replaced as Chief of Staff by General Erich von Falkenhayn.

THE BATTLE OF THE MARNE

THE OPENING days of August 1914 seemed to promise a fluid war of movement. While the Germans drove through Belgium, the French launched their own attack — Plan XVII — a headlong offensive in Alsace-Lorraine where German machine-guns mowed down thousands of men advancing in open order. However, as the German armies began to swing round into France, the Schlieffen Plan began to unravel. General von Kluck's First Army, on the extreme right, turned south-eastwards, exposing its flank as it marched obliquely across the face of the defences of Paris.

Kluck was now passing east, rather than west of the French capital. This movement was reported by British aviators on 3 September.

The information made little impact on the slow-thinking French C-in-C, General Joffre, who was shuffling his forces to the left to protect Paris and to meet the Germans head-on. But its significance was not lost on General Galliéni, the military governor of Paris. On the morning of 4 September Galliéni ordered General Manoury's Sixth Army to prepare to strike at the German flank and rear. Engaged by Sixth Army on the 6th, Kluck turned west to meet the threat, simultaneously opening up a dangerous 30-mile gap between First Army and General von Bülow's Second Army, which was now taking the brunt of Joffre's counter-offensive.

The BEF, which had halted its retreat, now advanced cautiously into the gap with the French Fifth Army on its right. The nerve of the German C-in-C, von Moltke, far away in his HQ in Koblenz, cracked as he cast an anxious eye towards the Channel ports and the threat to his rear posed by the (unrealized) intervention of fresh British armies.

On 9 September he ordered Bülow and Kluck to retreat to the Noyon-Verdun line. The Allies tracked them for five days before being halted on the Aisne by a hastily improvised line of German trenches.

Right: The shape of things to come. British infantry entrenched near St Marguerite in September 1914. The BEF had already fought from trenches on the Mons-Conde canal during the Battle of Mons on 23 August, a rearguard action in the face of the advancing German First Army which played a part in unhinging the Schlieffen Plan.

Above: The spoils of war. French troops pose proudly with German equipment captured during the Battle of the Marne. The battle had been fought along a front of some 300 miles by a total of some two million men. French casualties were 250,000 and the Germans about 200,000, a portent of future slaughter.

Right: The casualties mount. British wounded arrive at Charing Cross Hospital in 1914. British losses during the first four months of the war shattered its small Regular Army, leaving only a framework for the new volunteer and conscript armies that were to come.

THE RACE TO THE SEA

AFTER THE Battle of the Marne, both sides extended operations northwards, each trying to work round the other's flank. As this series of leapfrogging manoeuvres reached its conclusion, the BEF sought to deny the Channel ports to the Germans, crashing head-on into the Germans at Ypres on 20 October.

Such was the initial confusion among the British high command that the C-in-C, Sir John French, believed for at least 48 hours that he was attacking while his heavily outnumbered forces were barely holding their ground. His optimism gave way to something close to panic when he finally grasped the true nature of the BEF's position.

The British line held, supported by the French on their right. On the British left the Belgians opened sluice gates to halt the German advance. Bitter fighting on a narrow front continued until 11 November when torrential rain and snow halted the final German offensive. The First Battle of Ypres was the last chapter in the history of the old British Regular Army, of which nearly 80 per cent had been lost in the fighting. From the Channel to the Swiss frontier, both sides now began to dig in. Trench warfare had arrived.

Right: German troops march through the streets of Brussels on 20 August 1914. British and French withdrawals during the opening encounters meant that henceforth the war would be fought on French soil, nothwithstanding the qualified victory gained by the Allies in the Battle of the Marne.

Below: Figures in a landscape. British infantry cross a Belgian field in October 1914 as the BEF advanced towards Ypres. The Battle of Ypres was almost the last occasion on the Western Front when horsed cavalry was able to perform its traditional role of reconnaissance.

Field Marshal Sir John French (1852-1925), commander of the BEF from August 1914 to December 1915. A peppery veteran of the Boer War, and a noted womanizer, French showed excellent fighting qualities in the opening battles of the war, but failed to establish a good working relationship with his French allies. The scale of British losses in 1915, notably at Ypres and Loos, led to French's replacement by General Sir Douglas Haig.

TANNENBERG

I N A MILITARY convention with France, signed in 1913, the Russian Chief of the General Staff, General Jilinsky, pledged to put 800,000 men in the field by the 15th day of mobilization. On the outbreak of war, two Russian armies advanced into East Prussia, a tongue of land projecting across the River Niemen to the heart of Russia, flanked on the north by the Baltic Sea and the south by Russian Poland. Jilinsky's plan was for First Army, commanded by General Pavel Rennenkampf, to advance against the eastern tip of East Prussia while to his south, Second Army, led by General Alexander Samsonov, took the Germans in the rear, cutting off their line of retreat to the River Vistula.

The general commanding the German Eighth Army in East Prussia, von Prittwitz, panicked. He was immediately replaced by General Erich von Ludendorff who, lacking the rank to hold supreme command, acted as Chief of Staff to a nominal superior, General Paul von Hindenburg, brought out of retirement and squeezed into a uniform now too tight for him.

Even before Hindenburg and Ludendorff had arrived in East Prussia, the situation had been stabilized by one of Prittwitz's staff, Colonel Max Hoffmann. He had exploited the

Below: Cossack cavalry cut a dash for the camera. In August 1914 the Russian Army fielded 36 cavalry divisions. On the Eastern Front, which was never wholly deadlocked by trench warfare, cavalry had some freedom of manoeuvre. Over 4,000 cavalry charges were mounted on the Eastern Front, including the shattering of the Austro-Hungarian Seventh Army by Russian cavalry at Gorodenko in April 1915.

gap between the two Russian armies, separated by the Masurian Lakes, to mount a delaying action in the north while concentrating in the south against Samsonov, whose sluggish advance was spread over a front of 60 miles. Ludendorff finished the job by enveloping Second Army and taking 125,000 prisoners. The unknown number of dead included Samsonov, who committed suicide on 28 August. The Germans then turned on First Army, which fell back in disorder after suffering a crushing defeat at the Battle of the Masurian Lakes. German casualties in the two battles were fewer than 25,000 men.

Left: The victors of Tanneberg, Ludendorff (left), Hindenburg (centre) and Hoffmann (right). Their task was made easier by the Russian habit of sending their wireless messages en clair, code apparently being too difficult for them.

Below: Huddled masses. Captured Russian troops of Second Army after the Battle of Tannenberg. The German victory at Tannenberg ensured that German territory remained clear of Russian troops for the duration of the war.

THE TRENCHES 1

THE OPENING weeks of fighting had given the false impression of a war of movement. But in September 1914, as each side tried to outflank the other in the 'Race to the Sea', the first trenches — initially mere scrapes in the ground — began to make their appearance. Within weeks the stalemate they had produced on the Aisne spread down the 500-mile battle line from the North Sea to the Swiss frontier.

At first the picture they presented on the long, congealed front was by no means uniform. The Germans packed troops into the front line with little immediate support beyond some machine-gun positions. In contrast, the British, in the low-lying, frequently flooded coastal plain of the Yser, quickly dug a three-line system of front, support and reserve trenches linked by zig-zag communications trenches.

The British system set the basic pattern which troops endured for the next four years, from Flanders to the dry chalklands of the Somme and Champagne to the wooded terrain of the Vosges. Beyond the trenches, at a grenade throw's distance, lay the barbed wire entanglements, and beyond that the narrow strip which divided the opposing trenches — 'no man's land'. Its width varied from sector to sector, from as much as 500 yards to as little as 50. Near Zonnebecke in 1915 the British and Germans were only 10 yards apart.

Right: Men of the 42nd East Lancashire Division in a sap-head at Givenchy in January 1918. These positions, about 30 yards forward of the front-line trenches, were listening posts where at night sentries would strain to detect signs of enemy movement. The sap-heads were often built in shell craters. From 1916 a shell falling in no man's land would spark a series of bloody little battles as each side tried to seize the new crater and connect it to their own lines with a sap trench. Note the camouflaged persicope in the middle of the parapet.

Below: Men of the Royal Scots Fusiliers muffled againt the winter damp at La Boutillière in 1914. The white goatskin worn by the man in the foreground was an especially prized item. In wet weather the men's greatcoats could absorb an extra 35 pounds of water and caked mud. Added to 60 pounds of equipment, this turned the simple business of moving about into an ordeal.

Right: British troops share a trench with French infantry. The wattle revettements in the left foreground indicate that this is a French trench. The French avoided packing their front line, and thus leaving insufficient reserves to counter a breakthrough, by dividing the front line into what they termed 'active' and 'passive' zones. The former were strongly fortified and gave flanking fire to the passive zones on either side. The latter were heavily wired but lightly manned. Behind the front line was a network of shell-proof strongpoints and then a 'stop line' two miles to the rear, again divided into active and passive zones.

THE TRENCHES 2

A S THE war progressed, trench engineering became ever more elaborate. The German Hindenburg Line, built in the winter of 1916-17, consisted of three lines of double trenches to a depth of two miles, the first of which was protected by six belts of barbed wire, the densest of them 100 yards thick. Dozens of communications trenches linked the lines and to the rear were sited hundreds of guns zeroed to plaster 'no man's land' with shrapnel and high explosive or gas shells. Further forward, machine guns with interlocking fields of fire were positioned to strafe 'no man's land' the moment the enemy went 'over the top'. Railways were built right up to the rear areas to speed reinforcement and supply.

Living conditions in the trenches were often grim. During the wet season, they became morasses, particularly in the British sector on the Western Front. Men and mules could drown in the glutinous mud. Wounded men were particularly vulnerable. A survivor of Passchendaele recalled finding: '*A khaki-clad leg, three heads in a row, the rest of the bodies submerged, giving one the idea that they had used their last ounce of strength to keep their heads above the rising water. In another miniature pond, a hand still gripping a rifle is all that is visible while its next door neighbour is occupied by a steel helmet and half a head, the eyes staring icily at the green slime which floats on the surface almost at their level.*'

Above: Men of British 8th Division snatch exhausted sleep in a captured German trench at Ovillers during the Battle of the Somme in July 1916. A comrade keeps watch on the parados, the back wall of the trench. Note the firestep on the left, used by those on sentry duty or an entire unit when standing to face an enemy attack.

Left: On the Western Front two of the British soldier's greatest enemies were water and mud, the latter making even the shortest journey a nightmare. In July 1916 a Guards battalion lost 16 men through exhaustion and drowning in the mud. When an officer was ordered to consolidate his position, he replied, 'It is impossible to consolidate porridge'.

Above: German soldiers take time off in their dug-outs to examine their clothes for the eggs of lice, another scourge of the trenches, which caused frenzied scratching and carried a disease known as 'trench fever'. In 1917 it accounted for 15 per cent of all cases of sickness in the British Army. One British officer noted that 'captured German trenches on the Western Front sometimes had a species of small red lice crawling over their walls and blankets'.

Left: A pack horse loaded with trench boots struggles through the mud near Beaumont-Hamel in November 1916. Each British division was issued with about 2,500 pairs of these thigh-length gumboots. The Germans supplied thousands of waterproof overalls for men in the front line. A French officer wrote of these conditions: 'These days a sea of mud. The badly wounded are drowned as they try to drag themselves to the aid post. . . Dirty cartridges, rifles whose clogged mechanisms won't work any more; the men pissed in them to make them fire'.

THE TRENCHES 3

SANITARY CONDITIONS in the trenches were appalling. Rats gorged themselves on corpses lying in 'no man's land' or embedded in the walls of the trenches themselves. Trench foot and frostbite claimed about 75,000 British casualties during the war. On 'quiet' sectors boredom was a deadly enemy, although even here artillery, snipers and mortars caused a steady stream of casualties. During two months in the Neuve Chapelle sector in late 1916, the 13th Yorkshire and Lancashire lost 255 men although they had been on the defensive the whole time.

The tedium of trench routine was broken by the German dawn barrage and the Allies' reply at sunset, each side using the glare of the sun behind them to prevent the enemy from registering the position of their batteries. At night, patrols and trench raiding parties moved through the lunar landscape of 'no man's land'; wiring parties, burial details and re-supply detachments went warily about their business, keeping an eye open for star shell or enemy patrols, while the latest batch of wounded went 'down the line' to the rear.

Right: British troops savour the intimate fug of a rear-area dug-out, many of which were built in converted cellars in ruined towns and villages. Dug-outs varied hugely in size, comfort and security, from the scraped-out individual 'funk-holes' in the sides of front-line trenches to the often lavish accommodation provided in the German rear, which was provided with electric light, ventilation and solidly planked floors. Rear-area dug-outs were the deepest; the heavy artillery on both sides rarely bombarded front-line trenches for fear of dropping a near-miss on their own lines or undermining their own trenches.

Below: A German dug-out and its former occupant. An added danger of the trenches was posed by mines. Engineers on both sides dug tunnels under the enemy's lines in which huge mines were exploded just before an attack. When the British detonated 19 gigantic mines on the Messines Ridge on 7 June 1917, the sound of the explosions could be heard in London.

The British maintained morale with regular rotation between front, support and reserve positions, the arrival of letters and parcels from home and a concerted programme of recreational activities. However, experience in the front line was typically summed up in the soldiers' dirge:

> *'The world wasn't made in a day*
> *And Eve didn't ride on a bus*
> *But most of the world's in a sandbag*
> *And the rest of it's plastered on us!'*

Above: The battlefield at night. Shell fire, tracer flares and signal rockets frequently lit up the lunar landscape of 'no man's land' as trench raiding parties went about their business.

GAS

AT 5pm ON 22 APRIL 1915 two sinister greenish-yellow clouds crept across 'no-man's-land' towards the Allied lines at Ypres. They were pressurized chlorine gas released from over 500 cylinders in the German trenches as the preliminary to a major offensive. German prisoners and a deserter had warned of this new tactic, but no countermeasures had been taken. The two French colonial divisions on the north flank of the Ypres salient were engulfed by the cloud and fled in panic, leaving a four-mile gap in the front peopled only by the dead and those who lay suffocating in agony from chlorine gas poisoning. Having achieved total surprise, the Germans failed to exploit the breakthrough. Nevertheless, the gas had caused at least 15,000 casualties, 5,000 of them fatal.

Chlorine gas poisoning led to a slow and agonizing death by asphyxiation. On 25 September 1915 the British released chlorine gas on the German lines at Loos but little of it reached the enemy trenches. Thereafter increasing use was made of gas shells. Some 63 types of gas had been developed by 1918 but the most familiar was mustard gas, smelling like a *'rich bon-bon filled with perfumed soap'*, which literally rotted the body within and without.

The first countermeasures against gas were primitive, among them pads of cotton waste soaked in urine. The chlorine gas was partially neutralized by the ammonia in the urine. The famous box respirator did not appear until the winter of 1917 and soon became standard issue for troops at the front. Gas caused nearly a million casualties during the war, although this is only a conservative estimate.

Right: German stormtroopers burst through a cloud of phosgene gas, which had been developed in 1915. The poet Wilfred Owen, who fought with the Manchester Regiment, wrote of a man exposed to phosgene gas:

'. . .the white eyes writhing in his face,
his hanging face, like a devil's sick of sin;
If you could hear, at every holt, the blood
Come gargling from the froth-corrupted lungs,
Obscene as cancer, bitter as the cud
Of vile, incurable sores on innocent tongues."

Above: British machine-gunners protected against gas at Ovillers during the Battle of the Somme, July 1916. They are wearing grey flannel hoods with mica eye-pieces impregnated with phenol. A rubber-tipped metal tube was clenched between the teeth for exhalation.

Right: A German anti-aircraft crew in box respirator gas masks.

1915 – YEAR OF THE BIG PUSH

I
N THE opening campaign of the war the Germans had occupied much of Belgium and tracts of the industrial region of northern France. This enabled them to assume a defensive posture in the West while pursuing territorial ambitions in the East. The British and French had no such luxury. For them, the winning back of the territory lost in 1914 was a strategic necessity.

The British launched their first attempt to break the German line at Neuve Chapelle in March 1915. The battle saw a number of innovations: the extensive aerial photo-reconnaissance of the German positions; the co-ordination of artillery fire by timetable to fit the projected lines of advance; and the laying of an experimental network of field telephones before the attack went in. After a short 'hurricane' bombardment the British attacked on a narrow front with a numerical advantage of 35:1. They achieved an initial breakthrough before communications broke down, ammunition ran out and the advance stuttered to a halt – the pattern for future battles on the Western Front.

The British lost 13,000 men at Neuve Chapelle. In September, amid the slagheaps and ruined mining towns of Loos, they lost another 65,000 supporting a major French offensive in Champagne which suffered 190,000 casualties. There had been no strategic gain, only slaughter. In Britain, the shortage of shells caused a public outcry which led to the establishment of a Ministry of Munitions under David Lloyd George.

Below: A propaganda poster paints a heroic picture of Neuve Chapelle, but the casualty figures for the early summer of 1915 make grim reading. At the Battle of Aubers Ridge in May, 15 German companies and 22 machine-guns broke up an attack by three full British brigades. In an attack by the 1st Battalion of the Black Watch, only 50 men reached the German trenches alive. In the first two hours of the Battle of Loos, the 15th Division lost 60 per cent of its men. When 12 fresh battalions attacked on the second day – a total of 10,000 men – they sustained nearly 8,300 casualties. German machine-gunners watched as the British fell 'literally in hundreds'.

DESIGNED AND LITHOGRAPHED BY FRANK BRANGWYN, ARA   PRINTED BY THE AVENUE PRESS L™ BOUVERIE S™ LONDON ENG

AT NEUVE CHAPELLE

YOUR FRIENDS NEED YOU. BE A MAN

Above: Fraternization between French and British troops. Their sacrifice in 1915 had been in vain, but the French C-in-C, Joffre, remained confident that he was wearing the Germans down. However, the Franco-British offensives did little to distract the Germans from their business on the Eastern Front and the Balkans, where Serbia had been knocked out of the war.

Right: David Lloyd George, Minister of Munitions, and Winston Churchill, First Lord of the Admiralty, in Whitehall, October 1915. Both men were 'Easterners', wedded to the strategy of defeating Germany by an 'indirect approach' against her allies. In contrast, the soldiers to whom the politicians had ceded the overall conduct of the war believed that Germany could be overcome only on the Western Front, where her armies were the strongest. Lloyd George, who had originally opposed the war, had been appointed Minister of Munitions in June 1915, became War Secretary in June 1916, following the death of Kitchener, and Prime Minister the following December.

THE WAR OF THE GUNS

WITH THE arrival of fixed trench systems the war on the Western Front took on many of the aspects of a gigantic siege, requiring colossal quantities of all types of guns and projectiles. In August 1914 the first six divisions of the BEF fielded 486 guns, all but one of them light field pieces. By November 1918 the number of British guns in France had risen to 6,432 of all types.

During the war the British artillery loosed off over 170 million rounds, representing more than five million tons. During the two weeks preceding the Passchendaele offensive, in July 1917, British guns fired 4,283,550 rounds at a cost of some 22 million pounds sterling. At Messines in June 1917, the British concentrated 2,338 guns (808 of them heavy) and 304 large smooth-bore trench mortars on a nine-mile front, a ratio of one gun to every seven yards or 240 to the mile. In the 17-day preliminary bombardment, 5.5 tons of ammunition were delivered to each yard of enemy front.

Artillery accounted for up to 70 per cent of the casualties between 1914 and 1918. Troops subjected to heavy bombardment endured physical and mental torture. A French infantry sergeant likened the ordeal to being *'tied to a post and threatened by a fellow swinging a sledgehammer. Now the hammer is swung back for blow, now it whirls forward, till, just missing your skull, it sends the splinters flying from the post once more. This is exactly what it feels like to be under heavy shelling'.* Nevertheless, even after the heaviest bombardment sufficient soldiers survived to break up an infantry attack. The 4.3 million shells fired in the 14 days before the offensive at Passchendaele failed to suppress the defence. When the British went over the top, the German machine guns were waiting for them.

Below: An American heavy battery in action. The effect of persistent barrages was psychologically shattering. One British officer observed, 'Modern warfare reduces men to shivering beasts. There isn't a man who can stand shell-fire of the modern kind without getting the blues.' Another recalled that 'a barrage hung over us. It seemed as though the air was full of vast and agonized passion, bursting now with groans and sighs, now into shrill screaming. . . shuddering beneath terrible blows'.

Left: The sinews of war. Howitzer barrels swing over the shop floor at a war factory in Coventry.

Below: A British 60-pounder in action, March 1918, during the second Battle of the Somme. The 60-pounder also saw sterling service in Mesopotamia. Until the last months of the war on the Western Front, heavy bombardment often failed to destroy the enemy barbed wire, and by breaking up the ground created a new obstacle. In the Flanders plain, where the water table was high and the drainage system close to the surface, the results were disastrous.

THE DARDANELLES

I N OCTOBER 1914 Turkey entered the war on the side of the Central Powers. In Britain, operations against the Turks were considered necessary both to safeguard the Suez Canal and to relieve the pressure on the Russians by opening up a supply and communications route to them through the Dardanelles Straits, the passage from the Aegean to the Black Sea. A lodgement on the Gallipoli peninsula, on the northern side of the Straits, would also provide a springboard for a drive to Istanbul, forcing the Germans to withdraw troops from the Western Front. This was the argument advanced by the so-called 'Easterners', notably Winston Churchill, First Lord of the Admiralty.

A Franco-British naval attempt to force the Dardanelles in March 1915 came to grief on Turkish minefields. A hastily assembled expeditionary force of 80,000 men, commanded by General Sir Ian Hamilton, landed on the rocky coastline of the Gallipoli peninsula on 25 April. The Turks were taken by surprise, but Hamilton's timid generalship allowed them to rush up reinforcements and trap his men in their landing areas. The British element in the expeditionary force and the Australian and New Zealand Army Corps (ANZAC) were to be pinned down for almost a year. Trench warfare ensued, in conditions far worse than those in France. The British and Anzacs held no secure rear, only beaches exposed to Turkish shellfire. Everything – even water – had to be landed at night. Disease, particularly dysentery, took a terrible toll.

Above: The combined British and French fleet attempts to force the Dardanelles on 19 February 1915. The operation was suspended when on 18 March three capital ships were sunk and a fourth damaged by a combination of mines and shore-battery fire. World War I was the last conflict in which the battleship would be regarded as the main instrument of naval power.

Above: Turkish shells burst near the grounded *SS River Clyde* on 'V' beach at Gallipoli, 25 April 1915. The *River Clyde*, an old collier, had been converted into a crude infantry landing ship, with doors cut in her sides, but she grounded in water too deep for the men to wade ashore. Many drowned under the weight of their equipment. Under murderous Turkish fire, the sea ran red with blood up to 50 yards from the shore.

Two more landings at the beginning of August, offered a fleeting chance of a breakout from the beachheads, but the chance was frittered away. The troops were evacuated in December without a man being lost. The Dardanelles fiasco led to Churchill's resignation and the end of the Liberal government in Britain.

Below: A precarious bivouac for a British cavalry regiment. The stalemate of the Western Front was reproduced at Gallipoli, accompanied by the miseries of dysentery and enteric fever. The freezing weather in November 1915 produced 15,000 cases of frostbite.

Above: Anzacs in action. At 'Lone Pine Ridge' in August 1915, seven Victoria Crosses, Britain's higest award for gallantry, were won. At Gallipoli the British French and Anzac forces deployed finally numbered some 489,000. British casualties were 213,980, of which at least 145,000 were due to sickness. Turkish losses were as high as 350,000.

THE WAR AT SEA

WHEN WAR broke out, Admiral Beatty, commander of the Royal Navy's battlecruiser squadron, exulted, *'For thirty years I've waited for this day!'* The German High Seas Fleet did not oblige the flamboyant Beatty. Most of it withdrew to port. The losses the Germans sustained in the action off the Heligoland Bight on 28 August, when Beatty's battlecruisers sank three light cruisers and a destroyer, reinforced the German high command's reluctance to risk its battle fleet in the North Sea.

The German navy hit back on 1 November off the coast of Chile, where its China Squadron, commanded by Admiral Graf von Spee, destroyed a squadron of obsolescent British cruisers. Spee's success was short-lived. His two battlecruisers, *Scharnhorst* and *Gneisenau*, were hunted down and sunk off the Falkland Islands by a British task force led by the battlecruisers *Invincible* and *Inflexible*.

Meanwhile, the Germans continued to play tip and run in the North Sea. On 16 December their battlecruisers bombarded the coastal towns of Scarborough, Hartlepool and Whitby. Five weeks later, on 24 January 1915, on another sweep into the North Sea, a German force of three battlecruisers, five cruisers and 22 destroyers, commanded by Vice-Admiral von Hipper, was intercepted by Beatty's battlecruiser squadron. In the ensuing Battle of Dogger Bank the British sank the elderly cruiser *Blücher* and badly mauled the rest of Hipper's force before he slipped away.

Admiral Sir David Beatty (1871-1936), commander of the Royal Navy's battlecruiser squadron, 1913-17. Beatty led the action at Heliogoland in August 1914 and played an important part in the Battle of Jutland in 1916. He was appointed Commander of the Grand Fleet in 1917 and served as First Sea Lord, 1919-27.

Left: Britain's Grand Fleet, steaming in line ahead at the Battle of Jutland, May 1916. In the summer of 1914 it counted 20 dreadnought battleships on its strength, nine 'dreadnought-type' battlecruisers and 41 pre-dreadnoughts; 12 dreadnoughts and one battlecruiser were being built. In comparison, the German High Seas Fleet had only 13 dreadnoughts, five battlecruisers and 22 pre-dreadnoughts with seven dreadnoughts and three cruisers building. Thus the potential capital ship ratio was 42:28 in favour of the Grand Fleet.

Below: German survivors are picked up by the British battlecruisers *Inflexible* and *Invincible* after the Battle of the Falkland Islands, December 1914.

JUTLAND – CLASH OF THE DREADNOUGHTS

CONFRONTED with the numerically superior Royal Navy, Vice-Admiral Scheer, who had assumed command of the German High Seas Fleet, hoped to entice elements of the British Grand Fleet into a series of isolated actions in which the latter's strength would be worn down. However, the Royal Navy was able to anticipate the moves in this strategy thanks to the capture, early in the war, of the Germans' signals and cipher books.

On 30 May 1916, Admiral Sir John Jellicoe, commander of the Grand Fleet, learned via intercepted radio messages that the German fleet was sailing from Wilhelmshaven. In the vanguard was Vice-Admiral von Hipper's Scouting Force of battlecruisers and light cruisers, the bait to lead the British battlecruisers commanded by Vice-Admiral Beatty on to the guns of Scheer's battleships before Jellicoe could come to Beatty's aid.

Jellicoe set his own trap. Unknown to Scheer, his 24 Dreadnought battleships were steaming south from Scapa Flow on an interception course while Beatty's squadron of nine

Right: The man who could have lost the war in an afternoon – Admiral Sir John Jellicoe, commander of the British Grand Fleet. His indecision at Jutland aroused great controversy, but his prime aim was to preserve the Grand Fleet intact. His relations with his great rival Beatty were somewhat less than cordial.

Below: The battlecruiser *Queen Mary* (right) blows up at about 4.26pm. She had been hit several times and a cordite fire exploded her forward magazine. There were only 20 survivors of a crew of 58 officers and 1,228 men. Ahead of *Queen Mary* the battlecruiser *Tiger* is straddled by German shells. An observer in *Tiger* said of the end of *Queen Mary*: 'The whole ship seemed to collapse inwards. . . the roofs of the turrets [solid sheets of armour weighing 70 tons] were blown 100 feet high, then everything was smoke'.

battlecruisers, reinforced by four fast new battleships of the Queen Elizabeth class, sailed from Rosyth. Screened and supported by dozens of smaller warships, 37 British capital ships of the Dreadnought type were sailing against 23 of their German equivalents. It was the only occasion on which two modern battle fleets have engaged each other in European waters.

In the first clash between the battlecruisers, which began at 3.48pm on 31 May, at a range of 18,000 yards, Beatty lost *Indefatigable* and *Queen Mary*. At 5.26pm he turned back towards Jellicoe in an attempt to lure Scheer on to the guns of the Grand Fleet. Scheer swiftly executed a 'battle turnaway', in the process of which another British battlecruiser, *Invincible*, was sunk. In rapidly fading light the two fleets blundered into each other again at 7.15pm. Once again threatened with destruction, Scheer withdrew to the west under the cover of a massed torpedo attack by his destroyers which forced Jellicoe to turn away to the east.

When daylight came Jellicoe found himself steaming across an empty sea. The British had lost three battlecruisers, three armoured cruisers and eight destroyers; the Germans lost one old battleship, one battlecruiser, four light cruisers and three destroyers. The Germans could claim a tactical success but the strategic advantage still lay with the Royal Navy as the Grand Fleet remained in being.

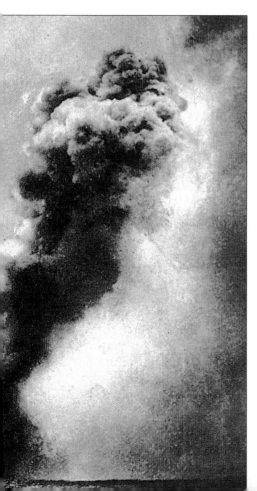

Admiral Franz von Hipper, commander of the German battlecruiser squadron at Jutland. The encounter demonstrated that the German ships were more battleworthy than their British counterparts, with heavier armour where it counted most and superior gunnery and fire control. At Jutland the Grand Fleet's largest losses in men and material were caused by inferior magazine protection.

THE BATTLE OF THE ATLANTIC

BY 1914 GERMANY had a submarine fleet of about 70 U-boats. German admirals, and their British counterparts, initially saw the submarine as an auxiliary to their main fleets, acting as scouts and harrying battleships. Little attention was given to the submarine's potential against Britain's merchant shipping lifeline.

At the beginning of 1915 the German navy stepped up its U-boat operations after the declaration of a blockade on the British Isles. Surface hunters forced U-boat commanders to make periscope rather than surface attacks, a tactic which made it hard to identify neutral vessels. On 7 May a U-boat sank the British liner *Lusitania*, among whose 1,200 passengers were 124 Americans. Fear of drawing the United States into the war prompted the Germans to bring a halt to 'unrestricted' submarine warfare in September 1915.

Below: A German U-boat at sea. Submarines posed a powerful new threat, but they were defeated by a combination of the convoy system and new technology. By 1918 the Allied Submarine Detection Committe had invented a new submarine-tracking sonar device named after it — ASDIC. Of the 372 U-boats deployed during the war the Germans lost 192.

Deadlock on the Western Front led to renewed demands for the reinstatement of unrestricted submarine warfare. On 31 January 1917 the Germans announced that all shipping, including neutral vessels, would be sunk on sight in the war zone of the eastern Atlantic, the measure which brought the Americans into the war. This did not unduly trouble the German high command, which had calculated that Britain would be starved into submission in five months, before US intervention could be effective.

The U-boats nearly succeeded. In April 1917, the month the United States entered the war, they sank over a million tons of shipping. The answer, forced on an unwilling Admiralty by the British Prime Minister, Lloyd George, was the convoy system. In the vastness of the Atlantic, 100 ships sailing in convoy, were as difficult for a U-boat to locate as a ship sailing alone and unprotected. Losses to the U-boats fell dramatically while those inflicted on the submarines by new minefields and packs of hunter vessels rose steadily. By 1918 the average life expectancy of a U-boat based on the Flanders coast was only six voyages.

Above: Victim of the U-boats. The solution to the U-boat crisis was the convoy system. An experimental convoy was run from Gibraltar on 10 May 1917, and by November the system had become fully operational, forcing U-boats to make underwater attacks. Convoy escorts were able to locate U-boats with the assistance of increasingly reliable hydrophones and attack them with depth charges. Mines were also improved and claimed many U-boats.

Left: Funeral service for victims of the sinking of the *Lusitania* by a U-boat in May 1915. The Germans claimed that the liner was carrying large amounts of war material in her cargo. There is convincing evidence that on her last voyage the *Lusitania's* hold contained millions of rounds of ammunition and a quantity of explosive.

KITCHENER'S NEW ARMIES

BEFORE 1914 Britain had not possessed a mass army of the continental type. But Kitchener, the Secretary of State for War, had the insight to grasp at the outset that the war would last for several years. Victory over Germany would require the raising of a 'million army'.

Kitchener launched a personal appeal to British manhood. Everywhere his stern face stared out from posters, declaring *Your Country Needs You*. The response was overwhelming. In the next twelve months, 2.3 million men joined what became known as 'The New Army'. Thereafter, with the flow of volunteers drying up, conscription was introduced for men between 18 and 45.

Below: Joining up in London's Trafalgar Square. Many who flocked to join the colours were under age. One volunteer recalled: 'The sergeant asked me my age and when told replied, "Clear off, son, come back tomorrow and we'll see if you're 19, eh?" So I turned up the next day and gave my age as 19'. Men not in uniform were often taunted and presented with white feathers as a mark of cowardice.

The immediate result was to leave Britain's industry short of skilled men, a factor in the shell shortage of 1915. So quickly had the New Army been formed that it had no uniforms, arms or equipment. Training bore little relation to the trench warfare being waged in France. The men of the New Armies got their first experience of the real thing in 1915, and were committed to action at the Battle of Loos in September of that year.

The new Army's inexperience had a baleful effect on British planning for the offensives of 1916. The New Army provided 97 of the 143 battalions which went over the top on 1 July 1916, the first day of the Battle of the Somme. Their commanders had no faith in their abilities. When the attack went in, no more was expected of them than a uniform parade-ground advance in successive waves across 'no man's land'.

Lord Kitchener (1850-1916), Secretary for War, 1914-16. Kitchener enjoyed wide-ranging powers, being both a minister and effectively Army chief until the curtailment of his powers after the Gallipoli fiasco in December 1915 when General Robertson was appointed Chief of the Imperial General Staff. Kitchener drowned on 5 June 1916 when the cruiser on which he was travelling to Russia struck a mine off the Orkneys.

Below: Doing their bit. Pupils at Eton drilling in 1915. Their time in the trenches would come.

VERDUN – THE CHARNEL HOUSE

IN THE winter of 1915 the attention of the German Chief of Staff, von Falkenhayn, turned to the French fortress system at Verdun, which had been virtually stripped of its guns and permanent garrisons. By forcing the French high command to defend this historic bastion to the last man, he hoped to *'bleed France white'* with guns rather than men.

On 21 February 1916 the Germans opened their assault with a bombardment of unparalleled ferocity. Four days later, as General Henri Pétain, arrived to command French forces in the sector, with orders to contest every shell-churned inch of ground, the virtually undefended Fort Douaumont fell to a patrol of Brandenburgers.

During the next three months no fewer than 78 French divisions went into the mincing machine at Verdun, fed down the only road not closed by German artillery, the 'Sacred Way', along which 6,000 trucks passed every day. The French stabilized their defences and the Germans began to substitute men for munitions. Now they were being bled white. By the end of April their losses were exceeding those of the French. The German effort was halted at the end of June, when the British bombardment began on the Somme and the Russians attacked on the Eastern Front. In the autumn, when the fighting at Verdun seemed to be over, General Robert Nivelle, who had replaced the promoted Pétain in April, launched a series of lightning counter-strokes which regained all the lost ground with very few casualties. Small consolation,perhaps, for the 500,000 the French had sustained in the defence of Verdun.

General Erich von Falkenhayn, Chief of German Staff, September 1914-August 1916, the architect of the strategy of attrition against the French at Verdun. His failure resulted in his replacement by Hindenburg, after which Falkenhayn commanded forces in Romania in 1916 and then in the Caucasus and Palestine.

Left: A French infantryman falls at Verdun. A French sergeant who fought in the battle described the agonizing effort needed to go over the top: 'What a hideous thing; to say to oneself, at this moment I am myself; my blood circulates and pulses in my arteries; I have my eyes, all my skin is intact, I do not bleed! . . . Oh, to be able to sleep thinking that it is finished, that I shall live, that I shall not be killed!'

Below: German prisoners taken at Verdun. Overall German casualties during the battle were 440,000. For French and Germans alike, Verdun 'meant hell. No fields. No woods. Just a lunar landscape. Roads cratered. Trenches staved in, filled up, remade, redug, filled in again. The snow has melted; the shellholes are full of water. The wounded drown in them. A man can no longer drag himself out of the mud'.

SACRIFICE ON THE SOMME

IN DECEMBER 1915 the British and French began to lay plans for a big joint offensive on the Somme, where their lines met. For most of the war this had been a quiet sector where battalions had, on occasion, drilled undisturbed on open fields in full view of the enemy.

After the exhausting struggle at Verdun, the burden of the fighting in this sector was to be shouldered by the British Third and Fourth Armies. Their extensive preparations were noted by the Germans, who strengthened their front-line defences to meet the attack announced by a massive bombardment which began on 24 June 1916.

The British high command confidently expected that the bombardment, which expended over 1.5 million shells – many of which were duds – would break up the German barbed wire, bludgeon their batteries into silence and entomb the defenders in their dug-outs. They were wrong on all counts. At 7.30am on the broiling hot morning of 1 July the bombardment moved on to the German second line. The German machine gunners emerged from their dug-outs, shaken but unscathed, to pour a withering fire into the 13 British divisions advancing at a walking pace across 'no man's land'.

Below: Irish troops rest in a communications trench on the first day on the Somme. Irish formations were heavily involved that day, and four Irishmen won the Victoria Cross, three of them posthumously. The Ulster Divison captured a long section of the German front line at Thiepval and fought its way through to the German second line before being driven back.

Right: Men of the Tyneside Irish Brigade going over the top near La Boisselle on 1 July. Advancing over open ground, the Brigade's 3,000 men were cut to shreds by machine-gun fire. Sergeant J. Galloway remembered: 'I could see, away to my left and right, long lines of men. Then I heard the patter-patter of machine-guns in the distance. By the time I'd gone another ten yards there seemed to be only a few men left around me; by the time I had gone 20 yards, I seemed to be on my own. Then I was hit myself'.

By nightfall the British had lost 60,000 men, 19,000 of them dead. The offensive ground on, making only minor gains. On 15 September British tanks were used to pierce the German line south of Bapaume, but there was no breakthrough, only autumn rain and seas of mud. The Battle of the Somme ended on 18 November, by which time the British had suffered some 420,000 casualties and the Germans a similar number. All idealism about the conduct of the war died on the Somme.

Above: British and German wounded on their way to a dressing station during the fighting near Montauban on 19 July.

THE HOME FRONT

IN 1914 there was a widespread feeling that, in spite of the war, it would be 'Business as Usual' back in Britain. In the next four years, however, the demands of war brought important social changes.

The massive exodus of men from the factories and mines to join Kitchener's New Army left Britain's industry short of skilled labour. In the factories their places were, in large part, filled by women, an important step on the road to female emancipation. During the war women moved into many areas of traditional male employment. A soldier returning to 'Blighty' on leave would be struck by women working on the railways as porters and guards and on the trams as conductors. Members of the Women's Land Army helped to boost agricultural output.

There were problems, however. In spite of government pledges, women war workers earned less than men. Trade unionists claimed that the employment of so many women in industry — in some munitions plants they outnumbered the male workforce by three to one — would lower mens' wages.

Below: A woman at work in an engineering factory. The war was a total conflict in that it forced the combatant nations to transform their societies, economies and even their political structures. It demanded the total mobilization of the state's resources on an unprecedented scale, which led to increased intervention in all aspects of its citizens' lives. This ranged from relatively minor matters, like the introduction of licensing laws and summer time in Britain — as ways on increasing agricultural and industrial output — to the direction of labour under the provisions of the Defence of the Realm Act.

During the war the price of staple foods climbed steeply. In 1914-15 the price of meat rose by 40 per cent and that of sugar by nearly 70 per cent, prompting accusations that 'profiteers' were exploiting the situation to make fortunes. Later the U-boat campaign threatened Britain's Atlantic supply lines, but the rationing of sugar, meat and butter was not introduced until February 1918. In 1915 the government acted more swiftly to introduce licensing laws, to restrict the hours when public houses could open, after it was claimed that well-paid munitions workers were drinking away their afternoons.

Below: The ration cards issued to King George V and Queen Mary. The King also attempted to set a good example to his subjects by giving up drink for the duration of the war and turning the royal estates over to crop production.

Below: Members of the Women's Land Army photographed in March 1918.

THE WAR IN THE AIR

THE SIMPLE statement, on the outbreak of war, that *'The squadrons flew to France'*, marked the end of secure British isolation from Continental Europe and foreshadowed a new form of warfare.

Sixty-three fragile but inherently stable aircraft of the Royal Flying Corps (RFC) accompanied the British Expeditionary Force. Their role, that of reconnaissance, was to remain the principal operational activity of the combatant air forces throughout the war. Air fighting began when bolder souls went aloft armed with carbines, darts and even bricks, to ensure that their duties were uninterrupted.

In February 1915 two Frenchmen, Roland Garros and Raymond Saulnier, experimented with a forward-firing machine gun, fixing steel plates to the propeller of their aircraft to deflect the small percentage of bullets they calculated would hit it. In April, Garros came down behind German lines and his captured aircraft enabled the Dutch-born aero-engineer Anthony Fokker to produce a mechanical interrupter gear, which allowed the gun to fire only when no propeller blade was in the way. It was fitted to the Eindecker monoplane, which thus became the first true fighter aircraft.

Right: RFC aircrew report after a mission over enemy lines. The spotting of targets from the air, and the ranging of artillery on them with the aid of airborne wireless sets, was the primary preoccupation of the Allied and German air services as long as artillery support was deemed essential in any attempt to achieve a breakthrough. The prevailing westerly winds placed the RFC at a permanent tactical disadvantage, taking a heavy toll of battle-damaged or malfunctioning aircraft struggling back to Allied lines.

Below: A British reconnaissance aircraft touches down at sunset.

Above: Aerial photography made rapid strides. By March 1915 the RFC had assembled a complete photographic picture of the German trench system opposite British First Army at Neuve Chapelle to a depth of 1,500 yards. Details of the German defences were traced on a map, 1,500 copies of which were issued to each corps taking part in the attack on 10 March.

ZEPPELIN

IN THE World Crisis, Winston Churchill wrote that from the beginning of the war there was a widespread fear that *'at any moment half a dozen Zeppelins might arrive to bomb London, or what was more serious, Chatham, Woolwich or Portsmouth'.*

In 1914 the German armed forces had 30 rigid airships, all of them of the Zeppelin type named after their designer Count Ferdinand von Zeppelin. Although their most effective role throughout the war was that of maritime reconnaissance, it was not long before the Zeppelins were employed on bombing operations, first on the Western Front and then against the British Isles.

The first effective Zeppelin raid on London was launched by the German Navy's Airship Division on 8 September 1915, when L13 penetrated London's primitive air defences to drop its bombs in a line running from Euston to Liverpool Street, killing 26 people. Following this, and later Zeppelin raids on London, much damage to property was done in anti-German riots. By the end of the war, 51 bombing raids by airships had been made against England, killing 557 people.

In spite of their size – the 'super-Zeppelins' introduced in 1916 were 650ft long – the airships proved fragile instruments of war, difficult to navigate with any accuracy, and vulnerable both to the elements and to fighters armed with incendiary bullets. By the end of the war over 60 of the German armed forces' 88 Zeppelins had been lost, 34 to accidents caused by bad weather and the rest to Allied aircraft and ground fire. Nevertheless, they exerted a powerful psychological effect and diverted significant resources to the air defence of Britain which would otherwise have been employed in France.

Above: Sentries guard the wreckage of Zeppelin L31, shot down over Potter's Bar on 1 October 1916 by a British BE2c piloted by Second Lieutenant Wulstan Tempest, who saw the airship's hull 'go red inside like an enormous Chinese lantern'.

Left: LZ95, a German Army Zeppelin used on the Western Front, where she was written off in 1916 after being hit by French shell fire and crashing near Namur. Note the forward gun turret on the upper hull, where the silhouetted figures indicate the huge size of the Zeppelin.

Right: Anti-German riots in London's East End after Zeppelin raids in the autumn of 1915.

THE FIGHTER ACES

IN THE hands of pilots like Max Immelmann and Oswald Boelcke, the Eindeckers took a heavy toll of relatively defenceless Allied aircraft. Boelcke, who claimed 40 victories, codified the basic techniques of air combat in a pithy set of rules for pilots, the 'Dicta Boelcke', which were still being issued, in booklet form, to Luftwaffe pilots in World War II.

Boelcke also drew on his experience in the fierce aerial fighting over Verdun in February-June 1916 to form specialized fighting squadrons, the Jagdstaffeln (hunting flights), known as Jastas. An early recruit to Jasta 2, commanded by Boelcke, was Freiherr Manfred von Richthofen, the top-scoring ace of the war with 80 victories.

With the arrival of new aircraft types, the Allies began to produce their own fighter aces, among them the frail-looking French Capitaine Georges Guynemer of Escadrille N3 and the RFC's youthful Captain Albert Ball, who flew with 11 Squadron. Like many aces they adopted 'lone wolf' tactics, undeterred by the frequently heavy odds against them. However, by 1917 air fighting had overwhelmingly become a matter of teamwork based on formation flying.

Above: Oswald Boelcke, the father of fighter pilot tactics. He claimed 40 victories before being shot down and killed on 25 October 1916 while leading Jasta 2, which subsequently became known as 'Jasta Boelcke'. Boelcke's contemporary fame was overshadowed by that of his friend Max Immelmann, the 'Eagle of Lille', who shot down 17 Allied aircraft in his Eindecker before meeting his end on 15 June 1916.

Left: The French ace Georges Guynemer, earthbound and surrounded by an infantry escort at a flag dedication ceremony. By 1917 the frail Guynemer was France's leading ace, flying Spad S VIIs with the elite Cigognes (storks) Group. He scored his 54th and final official victory on 6 September 1917; five days later he failed to return from a mission, possibly having been hit by ground fire. His Spad crashed during a barrage and both aircraft and national hero were obliterated by the shelling.

Left: The fabled 'Red Baron', Rittmeister Manfred Freiherr von Richthofen. He shot down more aircraft than any other pilot of World War I — 80 in all — and was a supreme professional in a new and deadly profession. He gained his nickname from the red-painted Fokker DrI triplane which he often flew and in which he was killed on 21 April 1918, shot down by a Sopwith Camel piloted by Flight Commander A.R. Brown of 209 Squadron, RFC.

Below: The Albatros biplanes of Jasta 11, von Richthofen's 'Flying Circus', which boasted some of the finest fighter pilots of the war. By the spring of 1917 the Albatros D III was being flown by all of Germany's front-line fighter units and was inflicting heavy casualties on the RFC. It was not until the autumn of 1917 that its performance was overhauled by new Allied fighters like the Sopwith Camel and the French Spad VII.

THE EASTERN FRONT

IN MARCH 1915 the Russians resumed the offensive in Galicia and took the great fortress of Przemysl. Their success forced the German Chief of Staff, Falkenhayn, to turn his attention to the Eastern Front. If he could decisively defeat the Russians, he could then bring superior forces to bear on the Allies in the West.

In May the Germans and Austrians attacked on a 28-mile front at Gorlice, driving the Russians out of most of Poland and taking nearly a million prisoners. The Russians held on, retreating 300 miles before halting the Germans on a new defensive line. The Tsar dismissed the Grand Duke Nicholas as Commander-in-Chief and took command himself.

In June 1916 the Russians were ready to attack again. Their drive on Warsaw came to grief, but south of the Pripet marshes General Alexei Brusilov unleashed a surprise offensive along a 300-mile front against the Austrian Fourth and Seventh Armies. Dispensing with a concentration of troops and a preliminary bombardment, he simply attacked wherever he could. In two weeks he took 200,000 prisoners.

Above: Tsar Nicholas II inspects a Cossack guard of honour. In 1915 the Germans put out feelers to the Tsar, suggesting a peace settlement on the basis of the status quo. Nicholas II, fearful that his authority might be undermined by anything less than total victory, remained loyal to his French allies. Russia remained trapped by the war, unable to win it and unable to escape from it.

Right: Russian infantry rest in a captured German trench. The Russian victories of the summer of 1916 were born of necessity. Lacking sufficient ammunition, Brusilov had relied on suprise, little or no preliminary bombardment and a series of separate attacks on a wide front to confuse the enemy as to his intentions. But he did not have the reserves to exploit the breakthrough.

Left: German troops march through a Russian town. In 1915, just as in 1914, the Germans achieved a series of spectacular victories on the Eastern Front, bundling the Russians out of Poland and taking 750,000 prisoners in the process. However, as General Brusilov demonstrated in the summer of 1916, the Russian Army remained a threat.

By the end of the summer, German reinforcements diverted from the attack on Verdun, and Russian shortage of ammunition and reserves, had shut down Brusilov's offensive. It had effectively undermined Austria as a military power but had also cost Russia nearly a million casualties, losses which accelerated the collapse which was to lead to the Russian Revolution.

THE ITALIAN FRONT

ITALY DECLARED war on Austria-Hungary on 23 May 1915. The main area of fighting was in the sector of the Isonzo River, west of Trieste, where strong Austrian forces were deployed in excellent mountain defences. The Italians battered away at them in a long series of offensives collectively known as the Battles of the Isonzo, but it was not until the eleventh offensive in August-September 1917, that they broke through the Austrian line.

German aid arrived in the form of Fourteenth Austrian Army, comprising mainly German troops, whose infiltration tactics secured victory in the twelfth Battle of the Isonzo, also known as Caporetto, in October-November 1917. By 12 November the Italians had been driven back to the River Piave, where the Austro-German advance was halted by a shortage of supplies and the arrival of 11 British and French divisions under the able General Plumer. Nevertheless, Italian losses were some 400,000 men, 350,000 taken prisoner.

Below: Italian gunners provide their Austrian opponents with a deadly form of Easter egg. By mid-September 1916, Italian artillery were pounding away in the seventh Battle of the Isonzo, which lasted well into November.

Below: Austrian troops in action on the Isonzo front. At the Battle of Caporetto, Austro-German forces used new infiltration tactics which drove the Italians back to the Piave. A young German officer who distinguished himself during the battle, winning a Pour le Mérite, was a certain Erwin Rommel.

German troops in Italy were transferred to the Western Front for Ludendorff's last throw in 1918, leaving the Austrians to punch themselves out in a renewed offensive launched in June. The Austrian-Hungarian empire was tottering into oblivion, and its high command desperately seeking an armistice in Italy, when at the beginning of November it suffered its final military defeat at Vittorio Veneto.

Below: German machine-gunners in Italy, 1917. The German helmet, the Stalhelm, was first issued to troops at Verdun in January 1916, but another year passed before it became standard issue. It weighed about two and a half pounds. The French helmet was introduced in 1915 and the British in February 1916.

THE NIVELLE OFFENSIVE

AFTER HIS success at Verdun, General Nivelle succeeded Joffre as the French C-in-C, promising to end the war with one swift blow of *'violence, brutality and rapidity'*. He found an eager ally in the British Prime Minister David Lloyd George, who enlisted Nivelle in his own private war with the British C-in-C, Sir Douglas Haig.

The Allied plans for a joint offensive in the spring of 1917, with the British high command reluctantly placing itself under French orders, was dislocated by the German withdrawal to the heavily fortified Hindenburg Line, which began on 16 March. Brimming with self-confidence which bordered on the pathological, Nivelle ignored the changed circumstances. His strategy remained unmodified when the offensive began on 16 April on a 40-mile front east of Soissons.

Before the battle began, Nivelle had predicted 10,000 casualties as the price of victory. In the first four days the French Fifth and Sixth Armies suffered 120,000 casualties. Nivelle's attempts to persist with his broken-backed offensive shattered the spirit of the French Army – already weakened by the sacrifices made at Verdun – and led to a widespread mutiny. Within a month, 54 divisions, half the French Army, could no longer be counted upon by its high command.

Right: The man who talked too much. General Robert Nivelle, still jaunty on a visit to New York in 1920. He made no attempt to preserve the secrecy of his offensive, and the Germans, armed with a captured set of French plans, prepared their defence in depth.

Right: French troops go over the top. In the opening phase of the Nivelle offensive they displayed great dash and courage in appalling weather conditions. But once again the German machine-guns had survived the opening bombardment to mow down whole waves of French infantry. The French gained four miles at the point of greatest effort, but no one believed that this was the decisive victory promised by the loquacious Nivelle.

Left: French prisoners of war after the Nivelle offensive. The effort they had made was about to prove too much.

MUTINY

IN THE spring of 1917, after the failure of Nivelle's futile offensive in Champagne, the French Army was rapidly reaching the end of its tether. For many units, leave had all but ceased and desertions had more than doubled. Pétain wrote gloomily, *'Hopelessness and pessimism spread . . . swamping as it did the mood of artificial enthusiasm whipped up from above . . .'*

In May 1917 isolated acts of protest and indiscipline flared into open mutiny. By the end of the month it was estimated that only two of the 12 divisions in Champagne

Below: At the end of his tether — a hero of Verdun. The ten-month battle took a terrible psychological toll. A young French officer killed at Verdun had written in his diary: 'They will not be able to make us do it again another day'.

could be relied upon – and none of those between Paris and Soissons. Astonishingly, the Germans remained unaware of the crisis gripping the French Army. The task of restoring order was given to Pétain, who employed a mixture of brute force and concessions. He restricted the death penalty to the worst offenders, of whom 55 faced the firing squad, although many more were summarily executed. He also formed disciplinary companies for those found guilty of mutiny, assigning them the most hazardous of duties.

Pétain also improved communications between headquarters and the men at the front, as well as increasing pay and enhancing conditions for his troops. Above all, Pétain put into practice his theory of wearing down the enemy with limited, inexpensive attacks. This package of measures hauled the Army back from the brink of disintegration and prepared it for the German offensives in 1918.

Below: French infantry in action in June 1917 at a time when few of them could be relied on to obey orders. By the end of May over 55 separate mutinies had swept through the French Army. The men who had not left their posts held the line but refused to attack. To cover their ally, the British were forced to continue their offensive at Arras, originally launched on 9 April as a diversionary measure in support of Nivelle's attack. The British 'diversion' eventually cost them 158,000 casualties.

Below: French infantry – the legendary poilus – examine their mail. The improvement of conditions at the front played an important part in rallying the French Army. On 2 June all troops were guaranteed seven days leave every four months, later extended to ten days. Food was improved as were the facilities in rest areas. On 3 August an order was placed for the immediate delivery of half a million beds to the rest areas.

THE GERMAN HOME FRONT

THE DEMANDS of war – its greed for guns and shells – created an industrial revolution. New industries sprang up to feed the war machine, and with them new systems of working and new social problems: food shortages and rocketing prices, resentment at 'profiteers' and the maintenance of the wives and families of men serving in the armed forces.

Germans blamed the food shortages they endured throughout the war on the distant naval blockade maintained by the British. Unlike Britain, however, Germany had imported little or no food before the war. The main problem was caused by the departure of millions of men from the land into the army. In 1916 there was a bad harvest followed by a bitter winter, the so-called 'turnip winter', in which root crops became the staple diet.

The food shortage concerned Hindenburg and Ludendorff, who by 1916 were the most powerful figures in Germany. Ludendorff presided over the establishment of a new body, the Kriegsamt, which organized the civilian manpower of Germany for war. In theory it could conscript all male labour between 18 and 60. In practice it bribed workers with higher wages.

But the food shortages haunted Germany to the end of the war. In October 1918 a member of the German government wrote: *'We have no meat, potatoes cannot be delivered because we are short of 4,000 trucks a day. Fat is unobtainable. The shortage is so great that it is a mystery to me what the people of Berlin live on. The workers say, "Better a horrible end than an endless horror"'.*

Below: Distributing bread in Vienna.

Left: In 1915, when hopes of decisive victory still ran high, crowds of civilians throng the Savings Bank of Charlottenburg as they subscribe to a War Loans drive. Each subscriber could hammer a nail into a huge wooden statue of Hindenburg. Significantly, none of the combatant nations attempted to pay for the war by raising taxes. Germany even reduced taxes to lighten the hardships of war. It was assumed that, in the final count, the defeated enemy would pay.

Below: Women and hungry-looking children join a ration queue in 1916.

THE YANKS ARE COMING!

WHEN Woodrow Wilson narrowly won a second term as US President in November 1916, the slogan of his Party, the Democrats, had been *'He kept us out of the war'*. However, American isolation was not to last much longer.

Unrestricted German submarine warfare drew the United States into the war. On 31 January 1917 Germany announced that all shipping, including that of neutrals, would be sunk on sight by U-boats in the Atlantic war zone. On 2 February Wilson broke off relations with Germany. The U-boats immediately began sinking US ships. Shortly afterwards, American newspapers revealed a German scheme, outlined in the 'Zimmerman telegram', to help the Mexicans recover New Mexico from the United States. Reluctantly, Woodrow Wilson declared war on Germany on 6 April 1917.

Below: General Pershing and George V inspect American troops. As the US military attaché to Tokyo, 'Black Jack' Pershing had observed the Russo-Japanese War of 1905-6. In 1916 he had commanded a force of 10,000 men sent into Mexico during the Mexican Revolution in pursuit of Pancho Villa. Pursuing the Kaiser as commander of the American Expeditionary Force was a more taxing undertaking.

Right: American troops receive a friendly welcome in London in August 1917. It would be many months before they went into action in France. At this stage in the war, American money loans were more useful than men. But the United States' entry into the conflict provided the Allies with a huge boost to morale and the hope of victory in 1918.

America's entry into the war brought almost unbounded manpower and material resources to the Allies, but it would take time for them to be mobilised. In France the American build-up was painfully slow. By 1 May 1918 there were scarcely eight US divisions in France, the bulk of them unprepared for action. Their commander, General John Joseph Pershing, wanted to form them into a separate Army Group and was reluctant to see his small force dissipated by detachments to help the British and French forces staggering under the impact of the Ludendorff offensive launched in the previous March.

Below: Baptism of fire: A confident column of American troops marches past battle-weary British infantry on 19 May 1918, ten days before US formations got their first taste of combat on the Western Front.

THE SIDE SHOWS

THE FIRST World War was a global conflict. The Central Powers, represented by Germany, Austria-Hungary, Turkey and Bulgaria, were eventually opposed by no fewer than 22 Allied countries, including Japan, Portugal and the United States.

The war spilled far beyond the Eastern and Western Fronts in Europe. Even within Europe there was the war between Austria-Hungary and Italy after the latter joined the Allies in May 1915. In October 1915, in an attempt to help the Serbs, an Anglo-French force landed at Salonika to open a separate Balkan front against Bulgaria. By 1917, nearly 600,000 Allied troops were tied down in this dead-end theatre, which the Germans sardonically dubbed the 'greatest Allied internment camp of the war'.

The Allied war against Turkey embraced the Dardanelles campaign of 1915, the Russian campaign in the Caucasus and the British campaigns in Egypt, Palestine and Mesopotamia. Campaigns were also waged in the German colonies of the Cameroons, Togoland and German South West and East Africa. In the latter, the brilliant German General von Lettow-Vorbeck, commanding only 4,000 men, tied down a British force of 140,000 in a four-year guerrilla war. A succession of frustrated British generals failed to get the better of Lettow-Vorbeck, who surrendered 12 days after the Armistice in November 1918.

Right: General von Lettow-Vorbeck (centre right), the German commander in East Africa, relaxes over a bottle or two of Bols. A commander of the highest calibre, Lettow-Vorbeck ran rings round his numerically superior enemy in a campaign in which the tropical, disease-ridden climate claimed the greater part of casualties on both sides.

Below: A battalion of Nigerian troops entrain at Lagos on 6 August 1914. They played a part in achieving a swift victory over German forces in the Togoland and the Cameroons.

Below: Serbian infantry outside Belgrade. The Serbian incursion into Austro-Hungarian territory ended in the autumn of 1915. In October, Bulgaria attacked Serbia. Under the combined weight of Austro-German and Bulgarian offensives, Serbia collapsed and her army took refuge first in Albania, then in Corfu. The Bulgarians went on to defeat the Anglo-French force in Macedonia and bottle it up in Salonika, where it was subsequently reinforced by the Serbian divisions from Corfu, the Russians and the Italians.

ENTER THE TANK

I N OCTOBER 1914 the official British war correspondent Colonel Ernest Swinton approached General Headquarters (GHQ) with a proposal to use the pre-war Holt agricultural steam tractor as a means of overcoming barbed wire and broken ground.

GHQ was not interested but Swinton's scheme eventually found a backer in Winston Churchill, First Lord of the Admiralty. In the autumn of 1914 armoured cars operated in northern France by the Royal Naval Air Service (RNAS) had enjoyed some success but had been hampered by trenches which the Germans had dug across the roads. The Admiralty's work on a solution to this problem coincided with Swinton's proposal and led to the establishment of an Admiralty Landships Committee in February 1915.

A series of trials led to a prototype armoured vehicle known as 'Big Willie' which was successfully tested at Hatfield Park at the beginning of 1916. Kitchener dismissed 'Big Willie' as a *'pretty mechanical toy'* but Haig was keen to use the machines – codenamed 'tanks' – in France as soon as possible. They were first employed in significant numbers on 15 September 1916, during the Battle of the Somme, but were thrown forward in uncoordinated fashion. It was not until November 1917 that the tanks were successfully employed *en masse* at Cambrai.

Below: Not the perfect weapon of war. A British tank abandoned during the Arras offensive in the spring of 1917. Only 60 tanks were available for the battle, and ground conditions prevented many of them from seeing action. To the end of the war the tank laboured under severe technical limitations. It was prone to mechanical failure, vulnerable to artillery fire and too slow to exploit a breakthrough. The Germans thoroughly distrusted tanks and made no significant attempt to use them until 24 April 1918, when they employed 13 at Villers Brettoneux. This action also saw the first tank-versus-tank encounter, when three British Mk IVs engaged three German A7Vs.

Left: Another casualty of the Battle of Arras. At Cambrai on 20 November 1917, the British used tanks en masse for the first time. After a lightning bombardment, 324 fighting tanks, using specially devised tactics, tore a six-mile gap in the Hindenburg Line. Once again, however, the breakthrough was not exploited and most of the ground gained was lost to a fierce German counterattack launched on 30 November.

Below: Mk V tanks and men of the Australian Fifth Division move up in the assault on the Hindenburg Line in 1918. The 'male' versions of the Mk V were armed with a short 6-pounder gun and a Hotchkiss machine-gun. Top speed was about 4.5mph.

THEY CALLED IT PASSCHENDAELE

ALSO KNOWN as the third Battle of Ypres, Passchendaele remains the symbol of the seemingly futile carnage of the Western Front and the obstinacy of the the British C-in-C, Sir Douglas Haig.

Learning nothing from the failure on the Somme in 1916, Haig now planned a purely British offensive in the Ypres salient, with the aim of driving to Ostend to capture the enemy's submarine bases and sever the Belgian railways on which German communications depended. Haig's intelligence staff voiced their misgivings about the waterlogged ground over which he was to fight, but on 25 July 1917 he informed the British War Cabinet that all was ready.

Below: A 9.2-in howitzer in action, November 1917. The Passchendaele offensive, officially known as the Third Battle of Ypres, took the form of eight separate attempts to extend the Ypres salient between 31 July and 19 November 1918. Siegrfried Sasson wrote of it:

> 'I died in hell —
> (They called it Passchendaele);
> my wound was slight
> And I was hobbling back, and then a shell
> Burst slick upon the duck-boards; so I fell
> Into the bottomless mud, and lost the light'.

Below: Infantry pick their way through the sodden earth near Pilckem Ridge on 16 August. Driving rain and strong German counterattacks through oceans of mud brought the first phase of the British offensive to a grinding halt.

The Germans had ample warning of the offensive. By the time the attack went in on 31 July there were nearly two million combatants crammed into the Ypres salient. Haig's preliminary bombardment destroyed the area's fragile drainage system and his 13 infantry divisions advanced into a morass. The attack ground on until the beginning of November, with progress being measured in hundreds of yards, before it was halted only five miles from the original start line. Each mile had cost 50,000 casualties.

Below: Australian troops at Château Wood. In September and early October masterful use of British artillery in step-by-step blows, and the vigour of Australian and New Zealand infantry divisions, made significant gains. Then the rain intervened again in drenching torrents turning the battlefield to porridge and forcing the abandonment of the offensive.

THE MIDDLE EAST

GALLIPOLI WAS not the only disaster the British suffered in their war against Turkey. At the end of 1915 General Townshend's advance on Baghdad was fought to a halt by stubborn Turkish resistance, and his force of 10,000 British and Indian troops bottled up in Kut-al-Amara. In April 1916 he surrendered. Baghdad was not taken until March 1917.

Greater success was achieved in Palestine, where General Allenby replaced General Murray as commander of British forces in April 1917. Allenby's instructions were to *'take Jerusalem by Christmas'*. This he duly achieved, entering the Holy City on 9 December.

In September 1918, Allenby renewed the offensive against the Fourth, Seventh and Eighth Turkish Armies (each of which was no larger than a division) under the overall command of the German General Liman von Sanders. At Megiddo, Allenby employed a brilliant deception plan, overwhelming air power and a strong cavalry force to achieve a victory which was not only comprehensive but also a rare example of surprise and mobility in a war dominated by barbed wire and the machine gun. Damascus was occupied on 10 October, and Turkey capitulated three weeks later.

Left: Irregular warrior. Colonel T.E. Lawrence, who in 1917-18 operated with a small group of other British officers alongside the Arabs against the Turks. Lawrence organized raiding parties attacking the Hejaz railway which isolated the city of Medina and obliged the Turks to divert 25,000 troops. The Arab Revolt laid the ground for Allenby's offensive of September 1918. Lawrence and his Arab allies entered Damascus at the end of the month. A complex figure, prone to fantasy, Lawrence was nevertheless a discerning theorist of guerrilla warfare, describing his exploits in 'The Seven Pillars of Wisdom'.

Above: RFC aircraft on an airstrip in Palestine in December 1917. Air power played an important part in the climax to the campaign in the Middle East. Having gained air supremacy over the German squadrons in the theatre, the bombers of the Palestine Brigade struck at enemy communications and headquarters. The Brigade's fighter-bombers then bombed and strafed enemy columns. Turkish Seventh and Eighth Armies were caught in defiles blocked with smashed guns and vehicles and then systematically destroyed. The Turkish Fourth Army, unscathed but in open country east of the Jordan, also took heavy punishment from the Brigade's Bristol Fighters, DH9s and SE5As.

Right: General Allenby enters Jerusalem, December 1917.

THE COMMANDERS

THE WAR threw up a number of formidable military figures but none of them was a commander of the first rank. All of them, however, laboured under two signal disadvantages. The First Word War was the only war ever fought in which commanders lacked voice control over their armies. Communications broke down almost immediately the troops left the trenches. The trenches themselves provided almost insuperable obstacles, not least because the commanders were caught by a fatal hiatus in the mobile arm. Horsed cavalry was quickly revealed as obsolete, while the tank had not yet been developed into the weapon which proved so decisive in the Battle of France in 1940. For most of the war defence was mechanized; attack was not.

On the German side, the dominating figure was that of Ludendorff, the victor of Tannenberg in 1914. He proved less successful on the Western Front from 1917, although his spring offensive of 1918 came close to success. At a lower level the Central Powers fielded excellent fighting generals in von Mackensen, the conqueror of Rumania; Liman von Sanders, who masterminded the defence of the Gallipoli peninsula in 1915; and von Lettow-Vorbeck, whose skilful defence of German East Africa against overwhelming odds earned him the distinction of being accorded the 'honours of war' when he was forced to capitulate.

Germany's warlords, Hindenburg and Ludendorff, in suitably forbidding mood. From 1916 they were the two most powerful men in Germany, symbols of the abandonment of the direction of the war by the politicians who had started it. Hindenburg served as President of Germany from 1925 to 1934, appointing Adolf Hitler as Chancellor in January 1933. Hitler became President when Hindenburg died in August 1934. Ludendorff was involved in Hitler's abortive Munich putsch in 1923 but later fell out with the Nazi leader.

Left: Pétain (left) and Joffre. The latter blocked the issue of steel helmets to the French Army in 1914 because he believed that the war would not last long enough for mass production to begin. Joffre was dimissed in December 1916 and shuffled off into the obscurity of an advisory role to the General Staff. Pétain succeeded the disgraced Nivelle as commander of the French Army and in 1918 became a Marshal of France. Pétain's postwar political career reached an inglorious climax as leader of the Vichy government during the German occupation in World War II.

Below: Haig and Foch in London in 1919. Foch, the dapper advocate of the offensive at all costs, and Haig, the monosyllabic political infighter, enjoyed a wary working relationship during Foch's time as Allied C-in-C in 1918.

For the French, Joffre's massive imperturbability, rather than any great insight as a commander, saw France through the first crises of the war. Pétain, the hero of Verdun, was a master of defensive warfare and a firm believer in wearing down the enemy with limited attacks, *'striking continually against the arch of the German structure until it collapses.'* In contrast, Foch, appointed Allied C-in-C in April 1918, remained the bristling spirit of the doctrine of all-out attack, although he was canny enough to sanction the use of a less expensive strategy in the summer of 1918.

Sir Douglas Haig, who succeeded French as the British C-in-C in December 1915, was a cool personality, virtually inarticulate at meetings, but a skilled political infighter with the ear of King George V. In recent years attempts have been made to rehabilitate Haig's reputation, but the fact remains that in 1916-17 his generalship cost the British Empire over 700,000 casualties to no discernible effect. His survival recalls the Tommys' melancholic dirge on the Western Front, *'We're 'ere because we're 'ere, because we're 'ere'.* Haig was there because he was there and no one better could be found to replace him.

REVOLUTION

B Y EARLY 1917 Russia's disintegrating war machine, and the huge losses it had incurred supporting its allies, had brought it to the brink of collapse. To war-weariness was added starvation in Russia's cities.

In March food riots in Petrograd (St Petersburg) coalesced into a widespread uprising which forced the Tsar to abdicate. In July a charismatic socialist, Alexander Kerensky, became head of a Provisional government committed to continuing the war. However, effective power in Russia's cities lay with the Councils of Worker's and Soldier's Deputies – the Soviets.

The capture of Riga by the Germans on 1 September brought the Russian giant to its knees. Thousands of troops threw down their arms and walked home. They had *voted with their feet*, as it was put by the Bolshevik leader Lenin, who in April had returned to Russia with German connivance, in a sealed train.

Below: The beginning of the end. An anti-war demonstration in Petrograd in February 1917. In January 1917 an English nurse serving with the Russians wrote: 'Sabotage – railroads destroyed, workshops looted. Mobs shouting "Peace and Bread". They are aware the war is at the root of their hardships. The Tsar wishes to please everybody and pleases no one. We are amazed at newspaper criticisms of the government. A few months ago the writers would have been arrested. Things cannot continue as they are'.

Unlike the embattled Kerensky, Lenin had no interest in defeating Germany or making the world safe for democracy. When the vacillating Kerensky finally moved against the Bolsheviks at the beginning of November, their Red Guards seized the Winter Palace in Petrograd and arrested the Provisional Government. Now in power, the Bolsheviks opened peace talks with Germany in December in the bleak Polish fortress town of Brest Litovsk. German forces were within 100 miles of Petrograd when, on 3 March, the Russian delegates signed a peace treaty, giving up Poland, Lithuania, the Ukraine, the Baltic provinces and Transcaucasia. Germany then moved 40 divisions to the Western Front.

Left: Alexander Kerensky, who tried and failed to induce the Russians to continue the fight against the Germans.

Below: They voted with their feet. Soldiers walking home from the front as the Russian army crumbled away under the impact of the last great German offensive on the Eastern Front.

THE BIRTH OF THE BOMBER

BY MAY 1917 the German Army had become disillusioned with airships and had developed a bomber capable of raiding targets in Britain – the Gotha GIV. An attack on the port of Folkestone on 25 May 1917 was followed by two dramatic daylight raids on London on 13 June and 7 July.

The raids caused a huge furore about the state of Britain's air defences, the rapid improvement of which soon forced the Gothas to bomb by night. Meanwhile the British set about forming their own strategic bombing force, which emerged in the spring of 1918 as the fledgling RAF's Independent Force, based in France and given the task of attacking German war industry.

The Independent Force's main weapon was the Handley Page 0/400, which had a maximum bombload of 2,000lb. Bad weather and demands for their use in a tactical role in the final Allied offensives of the war meant that the 0/400s flew only a fraction of their missions against German war factories. As the war drew to a close, frantic efforts were made to bring the massive Handley Page V/500 into service to launch 'terror raids' on Berlin, but the huge biplane never flew in anger. Bombing did little or nothing to alter the course of the war, but in four years had nevertheless achieved a degree of sophistication undreamt of in 1914, when pilots had gaily lobbed grenades from the cockpits of their aircraft on to enemy formations below.

Below: A range of bombs displayed in front of a German Gotha GIV bomber, an aircraft earmarked for the raids on Britain. Its successor, the GV, had a maximum speed of of 87.5mph at 11,483ft, an operational ceiling of 21,325ft, range of 520 miles and 700-pound bombload on operations over southern England. An unusual feature of the GIV and GV was the gunner's 'sting in the tail'; he was provided with a wide ventral tunnel which allowed him to fire downwards and to the rear, much to the discomfiture of air defence fighters attacking from this quarter.

Above: The Handley page V/500, the largest British aircraft of World War I, built to bomb Berlin. Only three were delivered before the Armistice, and total production was 35 aircraft. The V/500 had a 126ft wingspan and was powered by four 375hp Rolls Royce engines mounted in tandem pairs midway between the wings. It could carry 30 250-pound bombs on short-range missions or a 1000-pound payload to Berlin. It never flew against Germany but a single machine was used in air control operations on India's Northwest Frontier in 1919.

Right: Aircrew of the Royal Naval Air Service demonstrate the methods used to attack the Zeppelin shed at Dusseldorf in September-October 1914, an early example of strategic bombing. The hand-dropped missiles are 20-pound Hale bombs. On 8 October the Zeppelin shed and the fully inflated airship inside were destroyed by a Sopwith Tabloid flown by Flight Lieutenant R.L.G. Marix.

NEW TACTICS TO BREAK THE DEADLOCK

TO OVERHAUL military doctrine in the middle of an all-out war is a daunting task, but in 1917 the German Army rose to the challenge.

In the winter of 1916-17 the German high command adopted the concept of 'elastic defence in depth' on the Western Front. Manpower was reduced in the front line, whose defensive positions were simultaneously strengthened and deepened. This enabled a more mobile defence and offered the possibility of the tactical surrender of territory. Special counter-attack divisions were held behind these new defensive positions, the so-called Hindenburg Line, to which the Germans retired in February-March 1917.

New infantry tactics were developed. Realizing that frontal attacks in extended lines were horribly wasteful of human lives, the Germans trained storm troopers to infiltrate

Below and Right: German storm troops in action on the Western Front in 1918. They were supported by rapid and accurate artillery fire loosed off in hurricane bombardments. They bypassed enemy strongpoints, leaving them to be mopped up in the infantry follow-up. Theses tactics were aimed at achieving deep penetration with mobility maintained by means of sled-hauled machine-guns, horse-drawn light artillery and lorry-mounted observation balloons to spot for artillery. The advance was co-ordinated by an elaborate series of light signals. The storm troopers were also equipped with the new Bergmann light machine-gun which had been introduced in 1917.

enemy lines behind a rolling barrage, bypassing strongpoints.
These tactics, combined with the abandonment of a prolonged
preliminary bombardment, proved successful on the Eastern
Front in September 1917 during the
capture of Riga by General Oskar
von Hutier. They were employed
in the German counter-offensive
at Cambrai in the following
November, and were to play a
major part in the German
spring offensive of 1918.

Right: A throwback to medieval siege warfare — a
German flamethrower. Developed in Berlin in 1900,
the flamethrower used gas pressure to belch out
inflammable oil up to 20 yards. The weapon made
its first effective appearance near Ypres in July 1915,
when six flamethrowers were used against a position
held by men of the British 41st Infantry Brigade.

LUDENDORFF'S LAST THROW 1

TOWARDS THE end of March 1918 the Germans launched what they hoped would be a knock-out blow in the West. As Ludendorff put it: *'The situation in Russia and Italy makes it possible to deliver a blow on the Western Front in the New Year. Our general situation requires that we should strike at the earliest possible moment before the Americans can throw strong forces in'.*

The German high command hoped to drive a wedge between the French and the British, the former concentrating on the defence of Paris, the latter casting anxious eyes over their shoulders to their communications with the Channel ports. The attack, spearheaded by storm troops using Hutier tactics, began in thick fog on 21 March. The British commander, Haig, had correctly anticipated the offensive but had deployed most of his reserves in the north, risking the security of the thinly spread British Fifth Army – against which the main German blow was aimed on the Somme – in order to insure against a less probable risk to the Channel ports.

Paris came under fire from long-range guns on 23 March. On 2 April, Haig had to submit to the appointment of the French Marshal Foch as the Allied Supreme Commander. A week later, with the first German thrust running out of steam and ammunition, Ludendorff launched a second blow against the British in Flanders. On 12 April Haig issued his famous 'backs to the wall' order, forbidding withdrawal.

Right: Storm troopers crash past a fallen Frenchman in March 1918. By the time of the last great German offensive the French had almost exhausted their manpower potential; 100 divisions on the Western Front had been reduced to infantry establishments of 6,000, half the 1914 figure. If anything the British were in an even worse plight.

Opposite below: British wounded are marched to the rear through the streets of Saint Quentin, March 1918, during the second Battle of the Somme. The impetus of the German advance was slowed considerably by the looting and indiscipline of the infantry.

Below: German infantry train for the Ludendorff offensive at Sedan in February 1918.

LUDENDORFF'S LAST THROW 2

LUDENDORFF'S second blow nearly broke the British, who were initially denied help by Foch. But by the end of April the Germans had been halted at a cost to the British Army of 239,793 casualties in 40 days of fighting. The Germans had lost close on 348,000 men, prompting Ludendorff to write that his troops *'thought with horror of fresh defensive fighting'*.

Now running out of cards, Ludendorff mounted an offensive against the French Sixth Army in Champagne. It began on 27 May when 17 divisions stormed the Chemin des Dames ridge in the Aisne sector. This was to be a diversion before the final blow fell on the British. The Germans broke through and by 3 June were once again on the Marne, near Château-Thierry, only 56 miles from Paris.

Here the Americans made a decisive intervention. General Pershing rushed the the US 3rd and 2nd Divisions into action on the Marne, while 50 miles to the northwest, at Cantigny, the US 1st Division was thrown into the US Army's first offensive action of the war. For three days the Americans blocked the German advance at Château-Thierry and then counter-attacked with the French in mid-June after the Germans had been fought to a halt.

Right: An order arrives by field telephone at an American artillery battery near Château-Thierry.

Below: Ever ready but seldom used. British cavalry resting near Montreuil, May 1918. The Western Front had reduced cavalry to an anachronism. At the Somme in 1916 and at Arras in 1917, German machine-guns had wrought havoc with cavalry when they were brought into the attack. Ironically the tonnage of fodder required to maintain the BEF's cavalry and transport animals exceeded that for ammunition; between 1914 and 1918 the horses ate their way through 5.9 million tons compared with the 5.2 million tons of shells and bullets which crossed the Channel.

Ludendorff then delivered a double blow east and west of Rheims, supported by a great weight of artillery. In the eastern sector the French had made a tactical withdrawal and the Germans found themselves punching thin air. To the west they crossed the Marne on a three-mile front but German exhaustion, and plans for a crushing French counterblow, were about to wrest the initiative away from the German high command.

Above: Men of the US First Division, the 'Big Red One', in action at Cantigny, which they took on 28 May, an indication that a new force had entered the field. Small as this and other American successes were compared with the overall picture, it meant that the writing was on the wall for the German High Command. It had lost the race against time.

THE BLACK DAY OF THE GERMAN ARMY

O N 24 July 1918, Foch assembled the three Allied Commanders-in-Chief – Haig, Pétain and Pershing – at his headquarters. He told them, *'The moment has come to abandon the general defensive attitude forced on us until now by numerical inferiority and pass to the offensive'.*

The blow fell on 8 August. Once more the British attacked on the Somme, but this time their preparations had been concealed from the Germans with the greatest skill. Learning the lessons of Cambrai, the British and French avoided a preliminary bombardment and supported the attack with 462 tanks. Fog masked the initial thrust, which within 24 hours had driven 10 miles into the German lines. Ludendorff wrote: *'8 August was the black day of the German Army in the history of war'.* The Germans fell back on the Hindenburg Line after suffering at least 100,000 casualties.

On 11 August Ludendorff tendered his resignation to the Kaiser, who refused it but nevertheless observed, *'I see that we must strike a balance. We have nearly reached the limit of our powers of resistance. The war must be ended'.*

Right: Seaforth Highlanders clear a German dugout, August 1918.

Below: The 13th Australian Light Horse move up to the front on 22 August during the clearing of the approaches to the Hindenburg Line. This operation cost the British 190,000 casualties between 8 August and 26 September 1918.

Above: The wreckage of war. All that was left of the great Cloth Hall at Ypres by September 1918.

ST MIHIEL

IN SPITE of the Kaiser's prophetic words, the war continued. The final assault on the Hindenburg Line began at the end of September after a preliminary American operation against the St Mihiel salient, which had threatened Allied movements in Champagne since 1914.

Foch, the Allied Supreme Commander, gave the task to Pershing's US First Army. It was the first independent action undertaken by the Americans in the war. The attack was launched against the two sides of the salient on 12 September, combined with an assault against the centre by French troops. The Germans were caught in the act of leisurely retirement from the salient, and were bundled out by the Americans in the space of 36 hours.

The clearing of the St Mihiel salient was followed by the decisive Allied offensive of the war, the centrepiece of which was the breaking of the Hindenburg Line with a drive by French and US troops along the Meuse valley towards Mézierès and a British thrust east of the Somme. By mid-October, after heavy fighting in which the Americans suffered severe losses in the Argonne forest, the German Army was on the point of disintegration.

Right: Infantry of the US First Army attack German positions in the St Mihiel salient in the first independent action undertaken by General Pershing.

Above: A klaxon warns of a gas attack on an American position. The Americans suffered 58,000 gas casualties, nearly half of them caused by mustard gas. Its effects did not become apparent for up to 12 hours. Then it began to rot the body within and without, causing blistering and vomiting and stripping off the mucous membrane in the bronchial tubes. It might take a month for a man to die, strapped to his bed in excrutiating agony.

Right: American machine-gunners in the Argonne, a rough, thickly wooded region in which the Germans had prepared a defensive zone 14 miles deep. The inexperienced Americans took heavy casualties in the Argonne before they broke out into open country at the beginning of November.

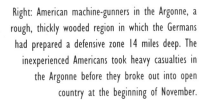

THE COLLAPSE OF GERMANY

BY THE beginning of October 1918, Germany's strategic position had been fatally undermined. One-by-one her allies had fallen by the wayside. On 25 September Bulgaria asked for peace. In Palestine, Turkish forces were in full retreat. In Italy the Austrian Army was on its last legs. On 27 October, Ludendorff resigned.

Inside Germany, hunger and a growing influenza epidemic were taking a heavy toll. In the port of Kiel 40,000 sailors mutinied. Austria and Turkey signed ceasefire agreements. On 9 November a socialist government seized power in Germany and the Kaiser abdicated. Since the night of 7 November a German delegation had been negotiating with Foch in his railway carriage headquarters at Compiègne. They had been instructed to sign whatever terms were offered. When they asked Foch what his terms for peace were, he replied *'None'*. The Germans admitted that they could not fight on. Foch replied, *'Then you have come to surrender'.*

At dawn on 11 November a message went out to all the Allied armies. The opening words were: *'Hostilities will cease at 11 hours today, November 11th'.* The guns were to fall silent. At first the men at the front could not come to terms with the quiet which lapped their positions. After over four years of war it was eerie not to hear gunfire somewhere. Relief came later, then jubilation.

Below: The face of defeat. German prisoners of war in 1918. At the time of the Armistice, on 11 November, the German Army remained unbroken but the political will to continue the war had evaporated.

Right: The meeting in a railway carriage where the Armistice was signed which ended the war. In June 1940, Adolf Hitler forced the defeated French to sign an armistice in the same carriage.

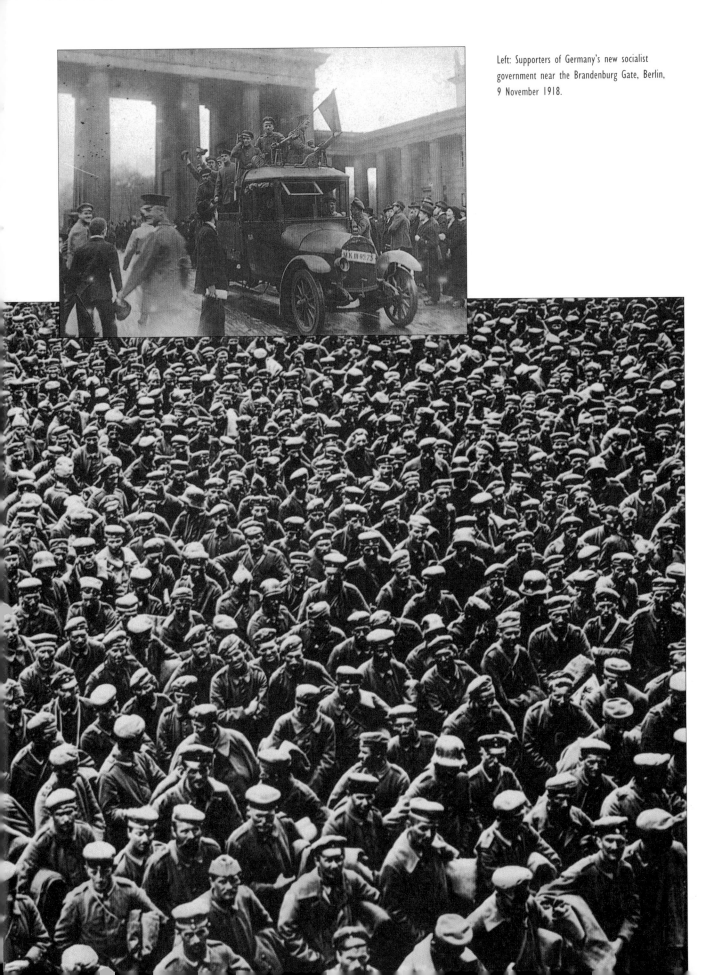

Left: Supporters of Germany's new socialist government near the Brandenburg Gate, Berlin, 9 November 1918.

AFTERMATH 1

I N THE summer of 1918 Germany occupied vast tracts of western Russia, containing one-third of her agricultural land and over half her industry. Through her Bulgarian and Austrian satellites, she controlled the Balkans. In the West, German armies were only 50 miles from Paris, having regained all the territory contested with France since the First Battle of the Marne in 1914.

Five months later the war had been won, not by the Germans but by the British, French and Americans. The German army, undefeated in the field and still numbering over 200 divisions, had effectively demobilized itself and marched home.

The feeling among Germans that they had been 'stabbed in the back' was increased when the victorious Allies met at Versailles in January 1919 to redraw the map of Europe, a task made all the more urgent by the collapse of the Russian, Austro-Hungarian and Ottoman empires.

Below: The Big Four at Versailles, Premier Orlando of Italy, David Lloyd George, the French Prime Minister Clemenceau and the US President Woodrow Wilson. In effect it was the Big Three as Orlando was confined to the sidelines of discussions, occasionally intervening to voice Italy's interests.

By the time of the Versailles conference a cloud of ambiguity hung over the Allied victory. The Allies themselves were now disarming. Although Germany was prostrate, and her very existence placed in doubt by revolution, her potential to rise again remained intact. To the French, above all, the securing of a durable peace meant the neutralization of Germany's potential by political or economic means. While the Germans considered the final terms, presented to them on 16 June, the Allies remained ready to resume war and the naval blockade on Germany stayed in place.

Below: British infantry raise their helmets to peace on 12 November 1918.

Below: The German fleet surrenders. The battleship *Friedrich der Grosse* sails into internment at the British naval base at Scapa Flow on 21 November 1918. The warships of the High Seas Fleet were later scuttled on the orders of their commanders.

AFTERMATH 2

THE TREATY was signed on 28 June. The numbers of the German armed forces and the arms they might bear were severely limited. Germany also lost all her colonies and much territory in Europe. France took Alsace-Lorraine, the Belgians Eupen and Malmédy, the Poles much of Posen and West Prussia. Danzig was to become a Free State and plebiscites were to decide the future of Upper Silesia, Schleswig and the Saar (which was first to have 15 years of international administration). The French were given control of the coal mines in the Saar to compensate for the German wrecking of their own mines in north-east France.

The east bank of the Rhine was demilitarized to a depth of 30 miles and occupied by the Allies for 15 years. The cost of this occupation was to be met by the Germans, who were also to make repayments for war damage to the tune of 6,600 million pounds sterling, a sum fixed by a Reparations Committee in 1921.

The treaty with Germany concluded the main business of the Versailles Conference, but work continued for the next 12 months on agreeing the boundaries of the states which were to emerge from the collapse of Austria-Hungary and the administration of large chunks of the Ottoman empire in the Middle East.

Below: The front page of London's Evening Standard tells the story of Armistice Day. An advertisement on the bottom right extols the virtues of a 'new custom of payment', by way of a cheque, which had become a commonplace transaction during the war years.

The 1914-18 conflict had ostensibly been the war fought to end all wars. The instrument by which new wars were to be prevented and peace maintained was the League of Nations, the formation of which had been the last of President Wilson's famous 'Fourteen Points' for peace. From the start, however, the League was hamstrung by the United States' refusal to join it. Marshal Foch, the Allied Supreme Commander in 1918, remained convinced that Germany would rise again. He boycotted the signing of the Versailles Treaty, observing with some accuracy that *'This is not peace. It is an armistice for 20 years'.*

Below: The debris of war: A pile of German steel helmets await destruction.

Below: Armistice Day celebrations in London, 11 November 1918. Winston Churchill remembered: '. . . I looked into the street. It was deserted. Then from all sides men and women came into the street. The bells began to clash. Thousands rushing in a frantic manner, shouting, screaming. Flags appeared. . . London streets were in pandemonium'.

COUNTING THE COST

I T IS impossible to estimate the final human cost of the war. The Russians suffered the most, losing as many as 3* million dead before the ravages of famine and civil war took their toll. The Austro-Hungarian empire lost at least 1.2 million dead and 3.6 million wounded, but these incomplete returns are almost certainly an underestimate. German figures are also uncertain; their own estimate was that they had suffered nearly 1.9 million dead and 4.3 million wounded. The French had total casualties of 5 million of which 1.4 million were dead or missing. The British empire suffered 3.2 million casualties of whom nearly a million were dead or missing. Of these some 745,000 came from the United Kingdom. Fighting on a narrow single front (with the exception of small contingents in Salonika and France) the Italians lost 460,000 dead. It is worth noting that this figure represents almost exactly half of the death toll of the entire British empire on all fronts. The Turks estimated their losses at 2.3 million, while the United States sustained 326,000 casualties, of whom nearly 116,000 were dead, 206,000 wounded and 4,500 prisoners or missing.

Below: The road to Chepilly strewn with men killed in the fighting of August 1918. The American poet Ezra Pound wrote an epitaph for them, and for those who survived:

> 'Died, some pro patria,
> non "dulce" non "et decor" . . .
> Walked eye deep in hell
> believing in old men's lies,
> then unbelieving
> came home, home to a lie,
> home to many deceits,
> home to old lies and new infamy'.

*Figures quoted in *The First World War* by John Terraine (Leo Cooper, 1983).